Leda

To Bushva

From KCM

Leda

K C MURDARASI

Matador
9 Priory Business Park
Wistow Road
Kibworth Beauchamp
Leicester LE8 0RX, UK
Tel: (+44) 116 279 2299
Fax: (+44) 116 279 2277
Email: books@troubador.co.uk
Web: www.troubador.co.uk/matador

ISBN 978 1780881 331

British Library Cataloguing in Publication Data.
A catalogue record for this book is available from the British Library.

Typeset in 11pt Adobe Garamond by Troubador Publishing Ltd, Leicester, UK

Matador is an imprint of Troubador Publishing Ltd

Printed and bound in the UK by TJ International, Padstow, Cornwall

For my Grandpa Allan, who believed in me.

Chapter 1

SUMMER 1992

The sun had only just risen when Leda woke up. The light coming through the thin curtains made her rub her eyes. On the sofa-bed opposite, her little brother Geni was still asleep. Leda slipped out of bed, pulled on her clothes quickly and started folding up her sheets. Her father would come soon for his breakfast and the room had to be neat before he arrived. At the other end of the room, in the bit that was a small kitchen, Leda's mother was making Turkish coffee in a tiny pan on the miniature gas burner. Her daughter could smell the dark, soft coffee powder from the other end of the room. She tipped the coffee into the water, then spooned in plenty of sugar. Leda knew how to make this coffee, too, but it never turned out as well as her mother's. Leda put her bedclothes away inside the sofa-bed, beside her spare clothes, and shifted the heavy wooden frame so that it settled back, with a clunk, into the shape of a sofa again. She arranged the sofa cover and the cushions and then, when she was sure that it was exactly how it should be, she went over to say good morning to her mother. The coffee was just boiling, the thick brown foam almost but not quite spilling over the edge of the pan as her mother lifted it off the flame.

"Good morning, Leda," she said, giving her a quick kiss on the cheek before pouring the coffee into two tiny cups.

"Good morning, Mami," said Leda. She started to go out to the well for a wash.

"Get some water for your father," her mother called after her. "He wants a shave."

Leda slipped on a pair of plastic sandals and walked down the porch steps towards the well. A mother hen scrabbled out of her way, squawking for her chicks to follow her. The well was near the house, and a bit further away was the toilet in a little hut. Leda washed her face with the water she drew from the well, then poured some more water into a plastic bucket, which she carried back to the house. Some water spilled on her clothes, but the day was already beginning to warm up, so she didn't mind. It was August, the school holidays and the hottest month of the year.

Back inside, Leda's father was up. She said good morning but he just grunted. Her mother poured the water into a pan to heat it. Leda started to get herself some breakfast, but her father rumbled "Enkeleda!" meaning he wanted her to bring his breakfast first. He sat down on the sofa next to the coffee table, since they didn't have a dinner table, and waited. Leda brought him a bowl of yesterday's bread and yoghurt, which he ate quickly and messily. Leda didn't say anything to him while he ate. He had called her by her full name, Enkeleda, which was a bad sign. He only did that when he was in a bad mood. Instead she waited until he had finished, cleared away his plate, and then started getting her own breakfast. Since there was no fresh bread, and yesterday's was hard and dry, she asked her mother for money and went out to buy some bread from the little village bakery.

Coming back with the bread under her arm, she saw her best friend Suela and called out to her. Suela ran over and kissed her on both cheeks. Suela had just been visiting her grandparents in another village, so she and Leda hadn't seen each other for two weeks when normally they would see each other every day. The sun had got into her hair, streaking its usual dark brown with gold, which suited her. Suela walked back to the house with Leda, telling her all about the journey and the things she had seen and done. She had been to the town, too, which was very exciting for Leda, who had not been since she got ill when she was little, and they took her to a doctor in the town. But the most exciting piece of news of them all was nothing to do with the town – it had happened right in Suela's grandparents' village.

"There were some foreigners there. They weren't from a different town, they were from a different *country*! They brought a big screen and set it up and then they showed a film on it, just like in a cinema! It was brilliant!" Leda had never been in a cinema, and neither had Suela, but it sounded wonderful. But the most amazing thing of all was what Suela said next: the foreigners were doing this in all of the villages in the area.

"Leda, they're going to come to *our village!*"

All this chatter meant Leda took a long time coming back with the bread. Her father had already left, and her brother was getting up. Her mother started to ask what had taken so long, but then she saw that Leda was with Suela and just smiled because she understood why Leda was late. She started to ask Suela questions about how she had enjoyed herself with her grandparents. Leda made breakfast for herself and Suela – bread with her mother's home-made butter, and boiled milk with sugar. Suela hadn't mentioned the group of foreigners to Leda's mother, and Leda didn't mention it either. She wasn't sure what her mother would think. Suela had told her that these foreigners were religious – Christians, she said – and Leda and Suela both knew that it was bad to believe in religion. They had been taught it in school. The leader of the country, Uncle Enver, had said many years ago that God did not exist, and so that was what everyone had to believe if they wanted to be loyal Albanians. Of course, he was long dead now, and just last year the Communist system of government, Uncle Enver's system, had been changed to democracy. At the time Leda had seen the riots in the capital city on the family's small television. They had pushed down Uncle Enver's statue in the central square of Tirana. It was a big statue, but on the little television screen he was the only person who looked the right size, and all the people pushing him down looked like little ants. Enver Hoxha was his real name, but Leda had been brought up calling him Uncle Enver, even though she didn't remember him at all.

Leda wasn't sure what she thought about the change from Communism to democracy. The television said that big changes were happening in Albania and opportunities were opening up, but they hadn't seen all that much improvement in their village. Instead, the factories in the town had closed down and a lot of her friends' fathers were out of work. Her own father had lost his job in the farming co-operative since the co-operative didn't exist any more. He worked as a day labourer now, cycling every day to a bigger village nearby and waiting for someone to hire him. He didn't always get hired. Leda's family ate meat even less often now than under the Communist voucher system, and never got new clothes, only mended and second-hand ones. But on the other hand, Leda was proud to be in a democracy – it sounded modern and exciting, like America!

And she knew that her mother was not sorry that she no longer had to get up at two o'clock in the morning every day to queue for milk! Neither Suela nor Leda knew whether the changes in Albania made it alright to have anything to do with religion now, so they kept quiet while they ate their breakfast, and just shot each other excited looks.

Chapter 2

For the next few days Leda could think about nothing else except the group of foreigners and their film. Every day she woke up wondering if they would come today. As it was the school holidays she didn't even have school in the mornings to take her mind off it. She helped her mother around the house, beating the carpets and choking on the clouds of dust that came out of them, or mopping the stone floor. She played with her friends in the streets or out on the hills. Once she went to the little travelling market when it came to her village to see all the new things which were coming into Albania, and bought herself some bright pink plastic hair grips with sparkles on for a few *lekë* – she had never owned anything so pretty before! A lot of the time she hung around with Suela watching her sheep. Suela's family had a small flock of sheep which her father took out to the hills every day so they could eat the grass. He had a huge dog to protect them from wolves and thieves. The dog didn't have a real name but Suela called it Lollypop because it was always licking her.

"Doesn't that make you the lollypop?" Leda asked, but Suela just laughed. Lollypop was almost as tall on all four legs as Suela and Leda were on two, but even though it looked very fierce it knew the girls, and they could play with it and rub its tummy while it lay on its back for them and tried to lick their faces. When they weren't playing with Lollypop Suela and Leda just lay in the shade and chatted, or dozed, or plaited the grass, and generally found a lot of different ways of doing nothing. It was on one of these mornings, when they were lying under the shade of an olive tree, that Leda saw the group of foreigners. The place where the girls were lying looked over the path to the village, and she could see in the distance a number of strange-looking people climbing up the steep hill. They were dressed oddly, some of them in shorts even though they were grown-ups, and some of them were carrying packs – one of those packs must have the film in it!

"Look, look!" Leda called to Suela, who was busy trying to make music with a blade of grass between her palms, and hadn't seen them.

"Is that them?" Leda asked Suela, who was the expert. Suela looked at them and burst into a big grin.

"That's them, that's them! Let's go and meet them!" They both got up and started to run towards the village. Panting as she ran, Suela said, "We'll...see...a film...tonight!"

Leda and Suela ran so fast that they got to the group of foreigners before they had reached the village. They ran from one person to the next asking questions – "Where are you from?", "What are you called?", "Have you brought the film?" – but the girls soon discovered that most of the group didn't know any Albanian apart from "How are you?" But with the group of foreigners were two young Albanians, and they told the girls that they would show the film in their village – but only if the village elder agreed. Did the girls know where he lived? Leda and Suela did know where the village elder lived. He was the grandfather of one of the girls at their school and he lived next to the small café he owned.

"We'll take you," volunteered Suela. "We know exactly where he lives, don't we, Leda?" She had to shove Leda to get her to answer, she was so distracted by all the strange new people. The Albanians turned to the foreigners and spoke to them in a strange language. You could tell that they were passing on what the girls had said, because when they heard it, the foreign men and women looked at the girls and smiled and nodded. Some of them even gave a "thumbs up" sign, which Suela and Leda didn't know the meaning of, but they thought it must be something good, judging by the smiles.

As they walked up the hill toward the village, Leda took the chance to have a good look at the strangers. There were eight of them, including the Albanians: five men and three women. The women were wearing skirts but some of the men had on the shorts Leda had seen from a distance, like the kind little boys wore. Many of them had T-shirts with writing in a foreign language. The colour of their skin was funny, much paler than Leda had ever seen. She wondered if they were ill, but they climbed the hill as if they were perfectly healthy. Two of the men and one of the women had blonde hair, and when she looked closely Leda could see that some of them had blue eyes as well. She had seen people with fairer hair than her own, and she knew that in the north of the country some people had blonde hair. She had seen blue eyes as well. There was a family in her village in which the husband and the youngest girl had blue eyes. But to see so much blonde hair and so many sets of blue eyes just in one little group! Well, that was just strange.

The group of strange-looking people certainly attracted

attention when they got to the village. As it was the summer holidays, none of the children were at school, so they all came to stare at the strange people, ran off to get their friends, and then came back to stare some more. It wasn't just the children, either. The old men playing dominoes in the shade watched them as they went past. Housewives came out of their doors and shouted to Leda and Suela, asking who the strangers were and what they were doing.

"They are foreigners, from outside Albania! We are taking them to see the village elder!" It was obvious how proud Leda and Suela felt to be the guides and companions of the foreigners. It was almost as if they had magicked them up by themselves, to judge by how their faces glowed and how high they held their heads as the walked along.

"Come on, come on," said Suela, even though she knew that most of the group couldn't understand. "It's this way, it's not far." Leda looked around at all the children staring at her and thought that even if the village elder didn't allow the film to be shown, it would still be wonderful just to walk along with the strange foreigners whose names she didn't even know, and feel special.

When they got to the village elder's house, his daughter-in-law had already heard that the group was coming and was waiting to welcome them in. They were shown into the living room, which was much the same as Leda's own, but a little more old-fashioned. There weren't enough seats for everybody. Suela and Leda sat on the floor. They weren't part of the group, but everybody in the village, when they saw them lead the group up the hill, had assumed that they must be connected with the foreigners, even if no-one knew how or why. The foreigners were talking a lot to the Albanians in the group, and the

Albanians seemed to be trying to stop them, or telling them to wait. Leda guessed that they wanted to start right away with talking about the film and why they had come, but this was Albania, and they were making a visit to someone's house for the first time, and things just didn't happen that way.

First, everybody had to be greeted by the village elder, and his wife and his daughter-in-law. There was a lot of hand-shaking and kissing on both cheeks. Then the daughter-in-law brought a tray of drinks in small, delicate glasses: strong spirits for the men, fruity liqueurs for the women, and fizzy drinks for the two girls. When the drinks were served it was time for toasts, welcomes and good wishes. The foreigners couldn't join in, or even understand what good things the elder was wishing for them, but the Albanians in the group returned the toasts, wishing the elder good health, long life, health for his children and so on. Then there were sweets and biscuits passed round, which everybody had to take, and the elder asked about their journey. And then, finally, they could start to talk about the important business – the film. Leda was all ears.

The conversation seemed to go very slowly because everything had to be translated, and sometimes two or three of the foreigners wanted to talk at once, and the translators didn't know which one to translate first. But slowly they managed to tell the village elder that they wanted his permission to show a film called "The Jesus Film". Leda had been hoping that they wouldn't tell the elder that they were religious, or that they would at least try to play it down, since she was sure that if anything would make the elder say 'no' it would be religion. But they were completely open about believing in God, even the Albanians. They even said that the reason they had come was so that people could learn more about their God, Jesus. Leda was sure the village elder would say no to the film after he heard that, and she prepared herself for the disappointment. Everybody in the room was watching the old man to see what his answer would be. When he spoke, he said something astonishing.

"I, too, believe in God. Hoxha was wrong about that. You may show your film tonight."

Leda was shocked. She knew she should be happy about the film, and she was, but she couldn't believe what the elder had said about God. Leda had thought that no-one believed in God – no Albanians, anyway – but now it looked like her own village elder had believed in God secretly all the way through the Communist times. Had Uncle Enver been wrong? What if God did exist? It was a lot to take in. She noticed that Suela was squeezing her arm, trying to get her attention. She managed to stop thinking about God and listen to what Suela was saying.

"We're going to see the film! You'll like it! It's got magic in it and everything!"

Chapter 3

When night fell that evening, Suela and Leda were in the village square. They had hung around with the group of foreigners all day, and had even helped them to rig up the screen they were going to show the film on. Now they were sitting on the ground, on pieces of cardboard they had brought so they wouldn't get dirty, and were waiting for the film to start. More and more people were turning up every minute, and there was a lot of noise from people talking. Leda had been told that her village was Muslim, historically, but there had been no religion for so long that it didn't make any difference, and most of the village turned out to watch the Christian film. All the children who were old enough to be out at this time had come. Most of them had never been to a cinema, so this would be the first time they ever saw a film on a big screen. People could hardly wait. The excited chatter was deafening.

At last, one of the Albanians from the group of strangers stepped up to the front and started talking. Leda couldn't always hear what he was saying, because people were still making a lot of noise, but he seemed to be talking about the person the film was about, Jesus, and saying that it was a true story. He said something about leaflets, too, but Leda, like everyone else, was impatient for the film to start and didn't really listen. Soon the speaker went to sit down and one of the foreigners (who had told the elder that he was from America) started to do something to the projector. It seemed to take forever, but eventually there was a noise and the big white screen lit up, shining its light on the faces of everyone watching it. The story started, and Leda was deaf to the noise around, unaware of anything except the wonderful screen with the people moving around even bigger than in real life.

The story it told was amazing, nothing like any story she had ever heard before. The hero, Jesus, wore strange clothes and had long hair – much longer than anyone had been allowed to have under Communism – and he did magic. But he seemed very kind and you could see in his eyes that he loved all the people who came to watch his magic and listen to him. Leda especially liked the bit when he let the little children come and sit on his knee after his friends had said that they shouldn't bother him. If she had been in the film, he would have let her come and sit with him, too. The man said lots of things about love, and some strange things about forgiving people and sin which Leda didn't understand.

But then the film turned horrible. One of his friends betrayed him for money, and he was arrested. Leda was sure that he must be let off, he was so nice! And if he wasn't let off he could do magic to get away. But it didn't turn out that way. The soldiers in the leather skirts killed him. Then Leda couldn't see the screen properly. It went all blurry because of the tears in her eyes. She decided she didn't like this film any more and started to get up to go away, but Suela grabbed her arm.

"It's alright!" she said. "It gets good again. He doesn't stay dead!"

Leda didn't know how Jesus could possibly stop being dead, but she sat down again, dried her tears and waited to see. And it turned out that Suela had remembered right. There was some more magic – God did it this time, the angels at the grave said – and Jesus came back just as alive as before, with only some scars on his hands to show what had happened to him. Then, after he had spent some more time with his friends (some of whom were women!) he sort of flew up to heaven. Leda supposed that was fair enough, since he had already died, and it was a much nicer ending than him dying. When the film stopped and the titles came up she clapped and cheered along with everybody.

Another person came to the front. This time it was one of the foreigners – a woman from England. Her hair was brown, cut short, but she had the same pale skin as the others. Leda listened a bit more carefully this time, wanting to find out more about the film and its hero, Jesus. The lady, through the Albanian translator, spoke about how she had first heard about Jesus when she was just a young child. She said that he was real and she knew him – that she had given her life to him when she was sixteen. Leda wasn't sure what she meant by "given her life to him", but the lady said that was what being a Christian meant. A Christian was someone who had given their life to Jesus. She said it was very important to have Jesus wash away all your sins. Leda wasn't sure if she had done any sins. She had lied a bit, and fought with her little brother, but they were just normal things, not proper sins.

It was as if the lady heard her thoughts.

"Even little things," said the translator, passing on her

words. "If you've lied, or stolen, if you've had nasty thoughts about your brother or sister, if you've been jealous. Anything that makes you less than perfect is sin. And God can't accept anyone who is less than perfect." Leda thought that religion sounded very hard in that case. After all, no-one is perfect. Once again, the English lady read her thoughts.

"None of us is perfect. But Jesus can take away your sins. Whatever you have done, he can wash it away and make you perfect because *he* is perfect. And he can give you perfect peace." There was a pause while the translator listened to the English lady, and then he turned to the crowd of Albanian villagers.

"Who would like to have their sins washed away? Who would like to invite Jesus into their hearts and give their life to him? Just put up your hands."

Leda thought for a couple of seconds, then put up her hand. It sounded good, if she really did have sins that needed washed away, and anyway, it didn't seem to cost her anything. She looked around and saw that she was not the only one with her hand up. Quite a few people had their hands in the air and were looking at the English lady and the Albanian translator with expectation.

"OK," said the Albanian man, "We are going to say a prayer. All those who put your hands up, pray this after us." And he prayed, and Leda and the others who had put their hands up repeated after him.

"Dear Lord."

"*Dear Lord*," they chorused.

"I am sorry for my sins and all the times I've done wrong things,

"I ask you to forgive my sins and make me holy,

"And I give my life to you.

15

"Please come into my heart and be with me forever. Amen"

"Please come into my heart and be with me forever. AMEN!" said fifteen people at once. Most of them, including Leda, didn't know what "Amen" meant, but she supposed it must be a special word that made the prayer work. She wasn't sure if she felt any different afterwards. She wanted to smile a lot, but maybe that was just because she had enjoyed the film. The people at the front were saying that those who had prayed should come and get a leaflet and a Bible, but Suela was pulling at Leda's arm, telling her to come back to her house for dinner, so she went with her friend instead. As they passed the big screen, one of the foreigners spoke to her. He must have seen her put her hand up. She didn't understand what he said, but he pressed a leaflet into her hand, and he seemed to really want her to take it. She put it into her pocket and said "thenkyoo", a word she had picked up from the foreigners today. He smiled, but Suela was pulling at her sleeve and she couldn't stay. She smiled back, and ran off.

Chapter 4

The years that followed that night brought a lot of changes to Albania, and some of them even started to reach Leda's village. She carried on going to school every morning and helping her mother round the house every afternoon. She carried on seeing her friends, especially Suela, and sometimes they would talk about the time the foreigners came with the film, or about Jesus, but that was less and less often as months and years went by. Leda's father managed to get a job as a van driver, so they were a bit better off. Some new things appeared in the shops – Coca Cola, sweets and chocolate, bananas, and most exciting of all, chewing gum! Some of her friends left when their families moved to the capital, or even abroad. Foreign films and soap operas on the TV showed how different the world outside Albania was, full of luxury and glamour. A lot of the older boys in the village started talking about leaving Albania, too, going to Greece or Italy, or even further. They couldn't get visas – these rich countries didn't want poor Albanians coming to live – but there was another way of getting there. Everybody knew there were fishing boats that took people to Italy, and as for Greece, well, that was just over the mountains. If you were fit, and brave, you could get there.

In ones and twos, the older brothers of Leda's friends started to disappear. Sometimes she would hear that they had arrived safely in the country they had travelled to. Sometimes they got caught and sent back, or couldn't make it over the mountains because of bad weather. Those ones usually tried again a bit later, especially if they had friends who had made it. There was one boy whose story was gossiped all around the village by tutting mothers and giggling girls. He had saved up all his money and paid a man with a boat to take him to Italy. They had set off just before nightfall from the port of Vlora, and had arrived just before dawn. The man wished the boy well and sailed away again. This boy, who was called Veisi, was so happy that he had made it to Italy that when he passed some people on the road he shouted out "Buongiorno!", Italian for hello. It was only when they answered in Albanian that he found out that the boatman had tricked him. He was still in Albania! They had just sailed down the coast all night. Veisi's story hung around the village for a long time, but he himself was gone. He couldn't handle the embarrassment and had gone over the mountains to Greece.

Eventually it became normal for families to have at least one relative abroad, and Leda, Suela and all the other villagers got to know the names of towns in Italy and Greece where whole communities of Albanians lived together, names like Bari, Lavrio and Thessaloniki. A few years before Leda wouldn't have known the names of any towns in Italy or Greece, except maybe Rome and Athens. But other than that, the emigration didn't really affect Leda's family; they just carried on as before – until the money started trickling in.

At first it was just a few families receiving a few euros from their sons abroad. Friends of their sons who had visas to travel to and from Greece would bring a bit of money from them, or the parents could open a bank account and their sons would put some money into the account in Greece. When money arrived they went out and bought some new clothes or shoes. Then more families started receiving a steady or steady-ish stream of presents from the boys abroad. The boys sent the money with instructions to buy things they had discovered abroad and now couldn't bear to think of their parents living without, things like electric kettles, fridges, heaters and reading glasses. One family sold their horse and cart and bought a car with the money from their two sons in Greece. Another old couple who had been horribly poor all of Leda's life, due to their eleven children, suddenly became one of the richest couples in the village when their nine sons went abroad. They bought some land and started to have a new luxury villa built. Eventually there was so much money being sent that a Western Union opened in the local town of Mallakaster, and then people didn't have to open complicated bank accounts or wait for people to come from Greece. There was some whispering round the village that the boys who were sending the most money weren't earning that kind of money doing honest jobs. People muttered things about drugs and guns, but nobody knew who had turned to crime and who was just working hard, so nobody said anything to the boys' families.

Leda was as amazed as everyone else at the new wealth coming into her village. She would go round to her friends' houses when they got something new, and would 'ooh!' and 'ah!' about the new wardrobe or kettle or duvet with real enthusiasm. She wasn't jealous, or only a little bit, and she didn't have any big brothers, so she couldn't wish that they were abroad and sending her money back. But it was different for her little brother Geni. He saw the new things, and it made him angry that his family couldn't afford things like that. Why did he have to shave with water from the well (he was fourteen now and had only just started shaving) when other families had hot and cold water inside the house? Why could they never go to the town for dinner in a restaurant on his birthday, or anybody's birthday? Why couldn't he wear cool clothes like the other boys instead of second-hand shirts and hand-knitted jumpers? He didn't say things like that in front of their mother or father because it would make them angry or upset, but he said them to Leda, and she told him to try and ignore it – there was nothing they could do. Some of his friends felt the same way, so they would hang around together and scowl at the boys who had brothers in Greece and wore jackets with labels on and cool trainers.

But it was when the emigrants started coming back for the summer that it all got too much for Geni. Some of the boys and men who had gone abroad had been granted permission to stay, since they were there anyway, and others had married Greek girls and got permission that way, so they could come back for the month of August to see their families. Even those who still didn't have visas would sometimes risk the trip over the mountains to see their families in the summer or at New Year. And when they came they came with money, lots of money. Some of them had flashy cars. Most of them had gold jewellery. They would drive into town and take their families or girlfriends to the fanciest bars and restaurants. Sometimes they would take trips up to Tirana, just for fun. Their clothes and trainers were the latest fashion, they had got tattoos and nice haircuts abroad, and they made no secret of the fact that they felt proud of themselves. When they drove their cars with their music blaring, everyone had to get out of their way, or else! When they went to a bar or café they expected to get served first, and they did get served first because the waiters knew they would leave a good tip.

Leda was in the house alone one day in the summer of '96 when Geni came in, slamming the door.

"I'm sick of it!" he shouted, using a swearword as well. He had started swearing about the time he started shaving, because he thought it made him seem older.

"I've had enough of those emigrants! They think they're better than us! They think they're better than me! Do you know what Ylli said to me in the café? He said 'Go home, little boy, you can't afford anything except Turkish coffee anyway.' 'Little boy'! He was only a few years ahead of me in school, and now he's been in Greece for two years and he calls me 'little boy'!"

Geni stopped ranting, took a breath and said, "I've had enough. I'm not taking any more of it. I'm setting off for Greece tonight!"

Leda wasn't sure what to say. She knew he couldn't really be serious; he was only fourteen years old. But if she acted as if he wasn't serious, that would only make him angry, and then he might go and do something stupid like running away. So she said, "Who will you go with?"

Geni looked surprised that she seemed to believe him.

"I'll go with Berti. I haven't asked him yet, but I know he wants to go. Tell Mami and Babi I'm staying with him tonight." He walked to the sofa and started rummaging through the clothes he kept inside it. He stood up with a few clean clothes in his hands, and Leda brought him a plastic bag to put them in. She slipped in his razor, too.

"You need a shave," she said. She knew it made him happy

when she said that. Most of his friends didn't really need to shave yet, and with his dark stubble Geni did look at least sixteen. Leda still didn't think he was really serious about going to Greece, but she thought she had better play along. He would just moan about the emigrants with Berti, and then come home tomorrow. She would pretend nothing had ever happened, and at the end of the month the troublesome emigrants would be gone. She kissed Geni on the cheek, and was surprised when he hugged her back, hard.

"You're a good sister," he said. "Take care of yourself, Leda."

Chapter 5

That night, Leda couldn't sleep very well. She dozed a bit, but she kept finding herself awake again, and thinking about Geni. She kept wanting to go over to Berti's house and find out if Geni was there, but they would all think she was mad, and she couldn't explain why she was so worried without getting Geni into trouble. She would just have to wait for the morning, but the morning was a long way away. She felt lonely, too, without Geni on the bed opposite her. She complained about his smelly feet and his snoring, but she was used to sleeping in the same room as him, and chatting a little bit in a sleepy way before one of them drifted off. The night was hot, and there were some mosquitoes buzzing around. Dogs barked outside, and further off a donkey was braying. She was used to the noises of the village, but tonight, because she couldn't sleep, they were getting on her nerves. She turned over again, trying to sleep, when all of a sudden she remembered something she had read a long time ago. It was something about being calm or peaceful, something like that. It sounded like exactly what she needed. Although it was a long time ago she could remember where she had read it – it was on the leaflet the foreign man had given her after the film about Jesus.

Leda hadn't read the little leaflet since that summer, and she didn't know if she still had it. It seemed silly to go digging around for an old leaflet in the middle of the night, so she spent a few more minutes trying to sleep, but it was obvious that she wasn't going to fall asleep anytime soon. She wrestled her way out of the sheet, which had wrapped itself round her legs, and lifted up the seat of the sofa-bed. She knew it must be somewhere near the bottom if it was there at all, so she pushed her clothes to one side and started rummaging. She hadn't switched on a light, so she felt around with her hands. She couldn't find any pieces of paper except some old jotters from school. She thought it must have been thrown away, and started putting things back in place, when suddenly her hand fell on something and she remembered where she had put it. She pulled out the photo album that was in her hand. She opened it, but all the photos were just black shapes, it was so dark. Leda knew that putting on the main light would wake her parents, so she walked quietly to the kitchen to get a candle and matches, and brought them back to the coffee table next to her bed. She lit a match, put it to the candlewick, and waited until it caught and then bloomed tall and bright. Now she could look at the album. Most of the album was photos of Leda with Suela or Geni, on their birthdays or at New Year, but at the back of the album Leda had slipped in some other things. There was a letter that Suela had written when she had been away at her grandparents' last year, a couple of birthday cards, a postcard with a character from her favourite soap opera, and, right at the back, the leaflet.

Leda pulled it out and held it in the candle's light. On the cover was a photo of Jesus, smiling like he did in the film. It said

"Jesus" above him in red letters. Inside there was information about how Jesus had died to save people from their sins, and there was a prayer a bit like the one Leda had prayed after the film. But there were also some lines from the Bible, and Leda scanned the leaflet, running her finger down the page, until she found what she was looking for: "You will keep in perfect peace him whose mind is steadfast because his trust is in you." She knew the "you" it was talking about was God. What Leda really wanted right at that moment was perfect peace so that she could fall asleep, and then it would be the next day and she would find out, she hoped, that Geni had been safe at Berti's all night. She slipped back into her bed with the leaflet in her hand, and prepared to pray.

"God," she whispered, "help me to trust in you so I can have perfect peace. Please let me sleep, and let Geni still be here in the morning, because…" she tried to think of some reason why God should do what she asked, but while she was still thinking she drifted off to sleep. She was woken by her mother putting away some dishes the next morning. At first she was all woozy from waking up and she didn't remember what had happened the evening before, but when she sat up she saw the leaflet lying on the floor where it had fallen out of her hand. Suddenly she remembered about Geni and Berti, and her prayer. God had answered her prayer for sleep, so surely that meant he must have answered her other prayer too! She got out of bed quickly, got dressed and was just about to go out in a rush when she realised how suspicious that would look. Her mother and father would want to know why she was suddenly so anxious to see Geni, since he had stayed over at Berti's lots of times before. So she washed her face, ate a small bowl of yoghurt, and then headed for the door.

"I think I'll go over to Berti's house and see what Geni is up to today," she said, trying to sound casual.

"That's fine," her mother replied. "Ask him if he's coming home for lunch."

All the way to Berti's house, Leda was twitching with nervousness. On one hand she felt sure he must be here – her prayer had worked. But on the other hand, she wouldn't be able to relax until she saw him with her own eyes. When she got to Berti's house she found Berti's mother, Mrs Stafa, frying eggs. The smell of vegetable oil filled the kitchen. Mrs Stafa looked round at Leda.

"Hello, Leda. It's very early for you to be over. Did Berti ask you to come and get something for him?" Leda's stomach suddenly felt very tight and heavy, as if she had swallowed a rock.

"What?" she said.

"Did Berti ask you to bring something back to your house? I noticed he forgot his comb when…" Something in Leda's pale, scared expression stopped her.

"Leda, what's wrong? Has something happened? Tell me!" So Leda had to tell her: Geni had said he was staying at Berti's house. It turned out that Berti had said he was staying at Geni and Leda's house. No-one had seen either of them since seven o' clock the evening before. Berti's parents came round to see Leda's parents, and there was some shouting and panicking, but no-one was at fault; the boys stayed over with each other all the time, how could anyone have known that they were lying this time? Only Leda had had any reason to be worried, and she couldn't say anything or all four parents would be furious with her, and anyway what good would it do? If they had set off for Greece last night it was too late for anyone to catch up with them. So she just stood around listening to them talk and argue and ask each other anxious questions, and felt totally sick.

After a while the adults were running out of things to say and people to phone for information, so Leda slipped away to be by herself. She went just outside the village, to the bank of the little river that ran down the hillside, sat down, and started to cry. Geni was gone! She might never see him again! Anything could happen to him in the mountains between here and Greece. There were wolves and bears, fierce sheepdogs, robbers and Greek soldiers. Even if he got to Greece he might get involved in crime, selling drugs or guns, and then he would change and he wouldn't be her little brother anymore. He was only fourteen! What was he thinking? Leda put her head on her knees and wept. She was angry at Geni, and at Berti, she was angry at herself for not stopping them, but on top of that she was angry at God. The first time she had ever asked him to do something for her, and he had let her brother go to Greece! What good was sleep if the worrying thing that stopped you sleeping came true? She dug the leaflet out of her pocket, ripped it in two and chucked it into the river. The pieces floated away, the two bits of Jesus' face swirling round and round before they disappeared over a little waterfall.

Chapter 6

Leda spent the rest of that August feeling miserable. The only person she could talk to about it was Suela, and Suela was visiting her uncle and his family in Tepelena, a town further south. As if feeling terrible wasn't bad enough, her father had reacted very badly to Geni's disappearance, and seemed to be determined to take it out on his family. He had always been a bit stern, but he had never been very strict with Leda and Geni. Now he had decided that Geni's disappearance was because he had not been firm enough as a father. Leda was the only child left, so that meant that she was the one who felt the effects of this new regime. Leda was hardly allowed to go out. The only time she was allowed out on her own was when her mother sent her to buy bread or milk, or some little thing from the local shop. She wasn't even allowed go to the vegetable market without her mother now, even though it was only ten minutes' walk away. Before, she had spent the long summer days outside the house, spending time with her friends down by the river or occasionally going to a little café if one of them had some money. Now she hung around the house and the yard, hoping that one of her friends would come to see her and worrying about Geni, feeling sick with guilt whenever her mother cried, as she often did, over her missing son. Friends did drop round quite often, but not as often as Leda would like, and their stories of the fun they were having swimming in the river and chatting to the emigrants in the village square made Leda feel more miserable. Her only treat was when one of her friends remembered to bring her an ice cream. The ice cream shop was too far away for Leda to go by herself, according to her father's new rules.

Leda couldn't wait for the end of the summer when she could go back to school again, to be with her friends and away from her mother's tears, but a nasty surprise was waiting for her. On the first day of term she got up and dressed early, so she would be in time for school, and she was just looking out her jotters and pencil case when her father came through from the bedroom.

"What are you doing?" he asked, surprised to see Leda looking ready to go out so early in the morning.

"I'm getting ready for school, Babi," she said.

"Oh, yes," he said, and laughed. Leda didn't like the laugh. What was so funny about going to school?

"You don't need to get anything ready, Enkeleda. You are not going to school any more. You are getting too old for it, and I don't like you spending so much time with boys, and with the kind of girls who will lead you into trouble. You are going to stay home and help your mother."

"What?" said Leda. "But I'm only sixteen, Babi! I'm supposed to go to school for another two years!"

"No arguments!" shouted her father. "I know what's best for you, and you are not going to school any more!" He stormed back into the bedroom, nearly knocking over Leda's mother, who was coming out. He didn't apologise to her. Leda's mother had heard the conversation, and from her expression Leda could tell that she had already known her husband's plans about Leda's schooling. But there was nothing she could do, so she just stroked Leda's hair and said, "It's alright, Leda. It will be alright." Then she hurried to put the coffee on, because Leda's father was coming back out of the bedroom. Leda sat on the sofa in a daze. No school! No going further than the corner shop on her own, and now her friends would have hardly any time to visit her. She thought about the weeks and months ahead, and she didn't know how she could cope with the boredom. She wondered where Geni was now, and hoped that his new life was turning out better than hers.

Life was boring after school went back, as Leda imagined it would be, but two things happened that autumn to make things better. The first one was that Suela came back from Tepelena. She was bursting to tell Leda all about her summer with her uncle and cousins, and she came round as soon as she got back. When she heard what Leda's father had said she found it hard to believe, too, but she soon started to make the best of it.

"I don't really like school, anyway; I think you're lucky. You were always cleverer than me, and I'm sure you'll still be cleverer even without school." Leda, who did like school, wasn't much cheered up by Suela's opinions, but she managed to persuade Suela to promise to bring round her school books sometimes, and tell Leda what they had been learning. The advantage of Suela's not being keen on school was that she was happy to spend whole afternoons with Leda when she should really have been doing her homework. Suela's parents didn't mind because she told them she was helping Leda study, which she sometimes was. Leda's father didn't mind because nobody told him. In fact

Mr and Mrs Kastrioti, Suela's parents, thought it was a shame that a bright girl like Leda should be taken out of school, but her father had the right to do whatever he thought was best for his daughter, so they didn't interfere.

The other thing that happened that autumn was that a Christian pastor started visiting the village. He came from a church in Mallakaster, the nearest town to Leda's village, but still not all that near. Leda heard about him before she saw him, since she couldn't go out of the house much. People said he was very young, only about twenty-six, but that he seemed very honest. He didn't look like an Orthodox priest, with black robes and a beard. He just wore an ordinary suit, and carried a brightly coloured Bible. Leda found out as much as she could about him. She was still angry at God because of Geni, but in spite of that – or maybe because of it – she longed to meet this mysterious person. She asked Suela constantly for news of him, until Suela started teasing and saying that Leda must be planning to marry the pastor, but like a good friend she did pass on the news when she had finished teasing.

A few weeks after he had started coming to the village, Suela said that a Bible study had started. The pastor had found some people who had become Christians when the film was shown, and other people who were interested, and they had all started meeting together to sing songs and read from the Bible. The leader of the little village mosque, which had re-opened after Communism, had gone to try and stop the pastor, but the pastor had stood up to him. He was polite, but he told the Muslim leader that the people had a right to come along if they wanted, and he wasn't forcing anyone. Suela said that people seemed to admire the pastor more since then. Everything Leda heard, as well as her boredom at being stuck at home all day, made her want to meet this pastor. She could tell him about how God had let her down, and see if he had any answers! She wouldn't pray, not since she had fallen out with God, but all the same she kept thinking that she *wished* God would let her meet the pastor, if that was possible.

Chapter 7

A couple of weeks later, God answered the prayer that Leda had told herself she wasn't really praying. She had gone to the market to help her mother. It was a cold, cloudy day in November. It had been raining and the sky looked ready to rain again. Leda's mother was trying to find some nice wool to knit socks for them all, and she had let Leda go and look at the make-up at a different stall to make up for her not getting out much. Leda was looking at the different lipsticks and face creams, and wondering if her mother would buy her something, as long as it was cheap. She was just rummaging through a basket of eye shadows when she was startled by a voice next to her. She turned round and saw a young man she didn't know smiling at her. He had thick, dark hair and a pleasant, almost handsome face, but he looked less tanned than a villager.

"Sorry, what did you say?" Leda said, wondering why he was talking to her.

"I said, you're Enkeleda, aren't you? The girl who doesn't go to school anymore. One of your school friends pointed you out to me," he said, seeing the surprise on her face. Leda looked behind him and saw her friend Alda waving to her. She was mouthing something. Leda tried to figure out what it was. Pasta, pasty..?

"Pastor! You're the new pastor!" she said suddenly. The man laughed.

"It sounds like you're telling me, not asking me. You've been doing some research?"

Leda blushed. "Well, I'd heard about you coming, and I don't know you… You are the new pastor, aren't you?"

"I'm not so new in Mallakaster. I've been the pastor of the church there for over a year. But I've only just started coming to your village, so yes, I suppose I am the new pastor." He seemed to expect Leda to say something to him, or ask him something, but she didn't. She certainly had things she wanted to ask him, but how do you ask a complete stranger in a busy marketplace about your missing brother? The pastor realised Leda wasn't going to start the conversation, so he tried.

"Your friend Suela seems to think you're a Christian."

"I am not!" shouted Leda. People turned round to look at her. She blushed again. "I mean, I sort of was. I prayed that prayer, you know. But I've never been to a church or anything, and the one time I ever prayed God didn't answer me."

She thought the pastor would be put off when he found out she wasn't really a Christian. That must be why he had come to talk to her. But he seemed to want to hear more.

"Tell me about it," he said. Leda looked at him in surprise, but he was being serious.

Just then her mother came back with the wool, and a light bulb to replace the one that had blown yesterday. She was surprised to see Leda talking to a man she didn't know. She shook his hand and they exchanged greetings, and then she looked at Leda, expecting her to introduce them.

"This is my mother, Mrs Bektashi. And this is, uh…" The pastor interrupted before Leda's mother could realise that she didn't know him.

"I'm Landi Rama. I'm the pastor of the evangelical church in Mallakaster." Leda's mother was a little surprised to hear this, but she just said "Pleased to meet you."

"Likewise, Mrs Bektashi. Now, I was just about to ask Enkeleda if it would be alright to come and visit her at your house. She has lots of questions about God, and I think it would be good for her education if I could explain the Bible to her a little." Leda didn't know whether to be pleased or angry. What did he mean, she had lots of questions about God? She did, of course, but how could he know that? And why did he want to talk to her about the Bible? She didn't even have a Bible! The pastor could see the confusion on her face, and he tried to hide a smile. Leda's mother didn't notice anything.

"Yes, I think that would be fine, Landi. I know Leda misses learning. She's finished school, you see."

"Well that's great," said the pastor. I'll come round when I'm next in the village, next week." Leda's mother explained how to find the house, and they said goodbye to each other.

As they were walking home, Leda's mother said to her, "Well, he seemed like a respectable young man. I'm not sure about too much religion, but it can't do you any harm to study a holy book. I'd heard there was a pastor coming to the village, but I didn't realise you had met him. Have you known him long?"

"Oh, no," said Leda. "Not that long at all."

When Suela came round that evening, she had heard about Leda meeting the pastor. She always heard first about everything that happened in the village. Since they had been such close friends for such a long time, Leda could see in Suela's face that she had heard about it, as soon as she stepped into the room. Her pretty best friend looked even prettier when she was excited by mischief or gossip. Leda's father was there, and she just knew that Suela would open her mouth, and then the pastor's visit would probably be banned and she would be in trouble. Her mother hadn't mentioned the pastor to her father, which meant that she thought the same thing – Leda's father would not be happy about it. Leda thought fast.

"Come through to the bedroom, you've got to see the wool my mother bought at market today! It's a really unusual colour." Mr Bektashi didn't take any notice – wool and colours and so on were for women to talk about amongst themselves. Leda grabbed Suela's arm and led her quickly through to the bedroom, and shut the door most of the way. She couldn't shut it completely or her father would wonder what they were up to. Leda pulled the turquoise wool out of its plastic bag, making as much crackly, plasticky noise as she could, and at the same time she hissed, "Don't tell Babi about the pastor! Please! I'll talk to you about him tomorrow."

Suela nodded, silently, and then said something about the wool being very nice. When they went back into the living room, Leda knew she was safe from her father finding out. Suela didn't stay long. It was obvious she had come round mainly to ask about the pastor. Since she still had her mind on that and couldn't talk about it, she thought it was best not to stay too long talking about things neither of them was interested in.

The next day was a Sunday and Suela was round first thing in the morning, just after Leda's father left for work. Leda's mother soon went out, too, to see a friend who was ill, so the girls could talk openly.

"Why did you tell the pastor I was a Christian?" Leda asked Suela.

"Well, you are, aren't you? I mean, you prayed that summer, and they said that's what makes you a Christian."

"Yes, but – that was private!"

Suela raised her eyebrows sceptically. After all, Leda had put her hand up at the film when almost the whole village was there.

"Well, not exactly private," she went on, "but I didn't want a complete stranger to know! He probably thinks I'll … I don't know, do whatever he expects Christians to do."

"Did he say he wanted you to do anything? He must know that you can't come to the Bible study," said Suela.

"Yes, he knows I can't go out. He said he wanted to teach me about the Bible and God."

"What's so terrible about that?" asked Suela, who still didn't understand why Leda was so angry.

"It's…" Leda sighed. "It's Geni, and the prayer not working. You know. I don't think I want anything to do with that kind of a God anymore."

"Well, I think Pastor Landi probably knows a lot more about this stuff than we do," said Suela. "I think you should talk to him. Why didn't you want your father to know, unless you actually do want him to come for a visit? If he asks you to do something, just say no and tell him not to come back again. But he seems so nice. I think you should give him a chance."

Chapter 8

The week seemed to go slowly for Leda. The days were getting shorter and the weather was getting worse. There were a lot of power cuts and they had to make do with candles. It rained for three days in a row and all the streets in the village turned to mud. Leda had to be careful when she went to the outside toilet not to slip in the slick mud that was everywhere, or step into a puddle in the dark. She helped her mother knit socks and jumpers, and she read the school books that Suela brought round, but she couldn't really concentrate on anything. She tried to cheer herself up by thinking about New Year, which was only a month away, but New Year without Geni would probably be miserable. Again and again she wondered where he was. She tried to picture him happy and healthy, living somewhere warm and safe, but she didn't see how that could be possible as an illegal immigrant. Sometimes she thought about him being hungry and cold, shivering in the streets with nowhere to go, and it made her want to cry. She wondered what the pastor would say about God letting Geni go away like that! In the end, a whole week passed and it came to the day for the pastor's visit. The moment she woke that morning, his visit was the first thing in her head, even though she had spent the whole of the day yesterday trying not to think about it. She spent that morning trying not to think about it, too, and surprised her mother by asking for more and more things to do around the house. Leda pretended to herself that she was not all that interested in his visit. After all, he had invited himself, she had never invited him! After lunch she found herself looking at her watch again and again, even though she tried to stop herself. She knew the Bible study was in the early afternoon from what Suela had told her, so he would probably come at three or four o'clock. As soon as it got to three o'clock, Leda could hardly hide her impatience. She opened a schoolbook and pretended to study, but she couldn't concentrate.

Suddenly, she heard the gate and footsteps started squelching across the muddy yard. She put the book down and got up to open the door. The pastor's smiling face was illuminated in the light from the doorway.

"Hello, Leda," he said. "How have you been?"

"Fine," said Leda. "Come in." Her mother came over to greet the pastor, and they asked each other polite questions about their health and the health of their relatives. Leda stood listening until her mother said sharply, "Leda, we have a guest! Go and get him a drink." Leda put on the plastic shoes and ran to local shop as quickly as she could in the mud. She got a bottle of Coca-Cola, which was a bit expensive, but they had an important guest. Normally they just drank water in the house. She promised to pay for the Coke later, and hurried back to the house. Her mother and the pastor were sitting on the sofa, talking about God.

"He doesn't waste much time!" thought Leda, as she poured the drinks. She took the tray over, along with some little biscuits. They all sat around for a while as her mother asked him about the church in the town, and how much the pastor was paid and so on. Then Mrs Bektashi stood up and said she would have to go and get the *byrek* out of the oven. She left Leda and Pastor Landi alone on the sofa.

So far Leda had said nothing to him apart from "Fine, come in." She wasn't sure how to open the conversation. What do you ask about God? Where should you start? She felt very shy and just sat fiddling with her glass. Pastor Landi didn't seem to feel shy or uncomfortable. He smiled at her and said, "Do you have a Bible, Leda?"

"No," she said. "I had a leaflet with some Bible verses, but…" She thought about the torn-up face floating down the river. "But I don't have it any more."

"I thought you might not," said Landi. He reached into the plastic bag he had with him and pulled out a large, colourful Bible like his own. "This is for you," he said.

Leda hadn't expected that. She took it and opened near the beginning. It was the story of someone called Abram, going on a journey. She flicked forward and found some poetry written by someone who was obviously very upset. He asked God to protect him from his enemies. Another flick and there was something about a terrible day of judgement. One more flick, and she found an old friend.

"Jesus!" she said.

"Yes," smiled the pastor. "You'll find stories about him in the books called Matthew, Mark, Luke and John. He's in other parts of the Bible, too, but these books are the ones in the Jesus film."

Leda looked up. "Have you seen the Jesus film, too? Is that how you became a Christian?" Landi explained to her that although he had seen the film later, he had become a Christian right after the fall of Communism. A lot of foreign missionaries had rushed into the country, along with Christian Albanians who had escaped from Albania earlier. They had come to his town, Mallakaster, and had told the people about Jesus. After years of Communist lies and threats, people were desperate to hear the truth, and Landi was one of them. He had been eighteen. He had been baptised in 1991, and a couple of years after that some missionaries had provided the money for him to study to be a pastor. He had spent two years in Hungary because there were no Bible schools in Albania, and when he came back he became the pastor of the church the missionaries had set up in Mallakaster.

Leda's mother had gone into the yard to feed the chickens and look for their eggs, which were sometimes very well hidden. The pastor looked seriously at Leda.

"Why are you angry at God?" he asked her.

Leda was stunned. How could he know that? After a few seconds she spluttered, "How did you know? I mean, why do you think that?"

"I could tell as soon as I asked you about being a Christian in the market. I think you have some secret grudge against God. But I know him, and I know that He doesn't hurt people unless it's for their good, so I think you have misunderstood him." Again, Leda was confused. Landi talked about God as if he was someone he knew, like Leda knew Suela. Did he really feel that way about God? She just stared at him for a while. He was the next to speak.

"If you don't want to tell me, you don't have to, but let me have a go at telling you. It has something to do with your brother who left. What is his name?"

"Geni," said Leda in a small voice.

"It's because Geni left. You didn't want him to. Maybe you asked God not to let him go, but he went. Is that about right?"

Leda started to cry. Without meaning to, she started telling Pastor Landi about how she was the only one who had known he was thinking about going, and how she had read the leaflet and prayed, and about how, in the morning, Geni was gone, and God hadn't done anything to stop him!

Pastor Landi listened sympathetically until she had finished. Then he said,

"How would you like God to have stopped Geni?" Leda looked up at him, surprised. She had never thought about it in detail before.

"I don't know, he could have … just made him not want to go, you know."

"But if God decided what Geni should think or want, he wouldn't really be Geni any more, would he?" he asked.

"I suppose not," said Leda. "But just that one time he could have done it. Or he could have made somebody see him and stop him, or something."

"He could," said Landi softly, "But how would you like it if, when you decided to do something, God stopped you? You wouldn't like it much, would you? You'd feel like a puppet with its strings being pulled."

"Not if it was something bad I wanted to do!" said Leda.

"Really?"

Leda thought about it. She preferred to think she would be sensible and be glad that she had been stopped from doing something silly, but if she was honest she knew that she would hate it. It wouldn't seem fair. She would feel just like Landi said, like a puppet.

"God doesn't want us to be puppets, Leda," he said. "God wants us to do the right thing because we want to, not because we are made to. It's not really being good if you're forced to be good. And God wants us to love him for who he is, not because he forces us to love him or serve him. That's why he doesn't force people to become Christians, they have to choose to. But it's a good choice."

Leda's mother had come back in and was wiping the dirt off the eggs with a cloth. Pastor Landi started collecting up his things to leave, but just before he got up he said quietly, "God could have done what you asked, you're right – but maybe he had another plan for that person. And all God's plans are good." Then he got up and said goodbye to Leda's mother. Leda put on the plastic shoes again and walked Pastor Landi to the front gate. She had a question she was bursting to ask.

"Pastor Landi, how did you know about Geni? Who told you?" Landi smiled at her.

"Praying isn't just you talking to God, you know. Sometimes he talks back!" Then he winked at her, and hurried off to catch the minibus back into town.

Chapter 9

Over that winter Leda started to really look forward to Pastor Landi's visits. During the week she would read the Bible he gave her, and she was always full of questions about what she had read when he came round again. He told her about the history of God's special people, the Hebrews, and how they had rebelled again and again and God had forgiven them again and again. He told her how Jesus' saving people was "Plan B", not because God had made a mistake but because without trying and failing so many times, human beings would never had believed that they couldn't save themselves. Landi showed her all of his favourite stories in the Bible: Daniel being saved from the lions, Joseph and his dreams about the future. And then, to show her that not all the people in the Bible were men, he got her to read the stories of Queen Esther, of Ruth and Naomi, and of Deborah the judge. Leda felt like she was really getting to know who God was, and she got to like him, too. And the Bible was just full of stories of people travelling to other lands and doing fine, which made her more hopeful about Geni. Pretty soon she started praying for Geni every night, which made her feel better, because now she was doing something to help him.

She told Suela about what she was learning in her lessons with the pastor, and she was so enthusiastic as she told her friend about what God had done, or what Jesus had said, that Suela laughed and said, "Nobody could ever say you're not a Christian now, not even you!"

"I suppose not," said Leda. "But you would be too if you read all this amazing stuff!" Leda's enthusiasm was so catching that Suela tried going to the Bible study a couple of times, but she said it was too much like extra school so she stopped. Still, she didn't mind Leda telling her occasionally about the new stories she had been reading with Pastor Landi.

Leda's mother was pleased to see her daughter looking so alive and happy again – even more than she had been before Geni had left. As with the schoolbooks, she just didn't tell her husband about the pastor's visits. She knew he would probably find out sooner or later, but she was sure that the lessons were doing Leda good, so she would deal with her husband's reaction when it came. In the meantime, she made sure she was always in the house or the yard when the visits took place, so that the neighbours wouldn't start talking about Enkeleda. After all, she was sixteen now, soon to be seventeen, and it wouldn't do for her to spend time alone with a young man.

As the winter wore on, and 1996 turned into 1997, with all the New Year presents and fireworks Leda had been looking forward to, her understanding of the Bible and of God kept getting deeper. She prayed every day now, not just for things that bothered her directly, but also for problems she heard about in the world. She saw prayers answered, too, like the time that they prayed the pastor would be able to come and hold the Bible study more regularly. The winter mud and snow had been creating big problems and the local minibuses were too old to get up the steep roads in that weather. Landi couldn't come on foot because he would get soaked and frozen, and if he got stuck somewhere on the road there were wolves that might come down from the mountains looking for a meal. God answered the prayer when one of the local drivers got a new, tougher minibus and, since his sister went to the Bible study, he never forgot to go to town on the right day to pick Landi up.

Pastor Landi had noticed that Leda was getting very serious about her Christianity. He started teaching her about more difficult and important subjects, about what would happen at the end of the world and how it was possible that Jesus' death could have taken away other people's sins. One day, he raised the subject of her future.

"Have you ever thought about Bible college, Leda?" he asked.

"No," said Leda, truthfully. The thought had never entered her head. When she thought about the future she thought she would probably end up the same as her mother, married and bringing up children. That was what her father wanted. College and things like that were for other people.

"But why?" asked Landi when she had explained. "It's obvious to me how much you love learning, and how much you love Jesus. You are exactly the kind of person who should go to Bible college! And there are plenty of colleges which take people who weren't able to finish school, like you." He paused and frowned a little.

"I know your father wouldn't approve, and you have to respect your parents, but don't rule it out. After all, anything is possible with God. It's time you started praying about your future, and we'll see what he comes up with."

Leda did think about the pastor's suggestion. She had plenty of spare time to think, and she wondered what it would be like to be a student, and to spend all her time learning about God and the Bible. Sometimes she thought it sounded wonderful, and at other times she couldn't imagine sitting exams about Jesus – he had started to feel like her friend now, not like a school subject. But on the whole she thought it sounded great, and the future seemed so much wider and full of possibilities when she let herself believe that she could go to Bible college. It was a dream that kept her happy during the miserable winter days, but she never mentioned it to her parents because she knew that they would never let her, and then her dream would be lost.

She could mention it to Suela, of course, but the next time Suela came she had some news of her own – she was going to Tepelena again. Her uncle had asked her parents to let her go again, and they had agreed, which was quite surprising. Suela was thrilled, especially as it would mean time off school. The weather was just beginning to pick up, the snow was starting to melt and spring would soon be on the way. It looked like the perfect time for a holiday. She had another reason for being so keen, which she whispered to Leda when she was sure there was no one listening.

"I bet it's because of Maks. You know, he's my uncle's wife's nephew, he lives in Italy. He was there in the summer, and I think he liked me – you know, *really* liked me! I bet he's come back and wants to see me again. What if he proposes?!"

"Calm down," said Leda, laughing. "Even if Maks is there, it's a bit fast for him to be proposing. You hardly know him, and he hasn't even met your parents, has he?"

"No," admitted Suela, "But he is very handsome and very rich. And just imagine living in Italy! I hope this is because of Maks!"

Suela was so excited about the trip to Tepelena that Leda didn't really know how to tell her about her dream of going to Bible college. When she eventually mentioned what Pastor Landi had said, Suela laughed.

"You're crazy! More school?" But when she saw that she had hurt Leda's feelings, she started being more serious.

"You'd be really good at it, I'm not saying it's a stupid idea. And if that's what you want to do then I hope you get to do it. But I don't think your babi would ever let you, Leda." She thought hard for a minute. "I think you'd better just pray about it like the pastor said. He seems to think that works. Who knows, maybe you can come to Italy to study and stay with me and my gorgeous husband Maks!" That started Leda off laughing, and they kept having fits of the giggles for the rest of the afternoon whenever they caught each other's eye.

When Suela had to go they calmed down a bit because it would be the last time they would see each other before she went away to Tepelena. Leda knew she would be lonely without her best friend, and she could be gone a month or two, but she wanted to be cheerful because Suela was so happy.

"You go and have a good time with your cousins, and with you-know-who! I'll be praying for you."

"Thanks, Leda," said Suela. "I'll phone you and let you know what I'm up to." Then they kissed each other, and Suela walked home through the dim light of a February evening.

Chapter 10

Suela didn't phone the first week, or the second week. Leda supposed she must be too busy having fun in Tepelena. She wished she could go to Tepelena, too, but her father still wouldn't let her go any further than the end of the road. She had tried talking to him about the strict rules, but he would never discuss it. Once in a while her parents would let her phone Suela's uncle's house, but Suela was never there and although Leda left messages, her friend never phoned back. Leda heard news about Suela, though, from her parents and from her other friends who had picked up gossip. It seemed that Maks *had* come over from Italy, and he did want to marry Suela. The word was that they were planning to marry very soon, in only a few weeks! Leda was very surprised, and a bit worried. She hoped Suela knew what she was doing.

But pretty soon Leda had too many problems of her own to worry about Suela's for her. She had become so used to Pastor Landi's visits that she had almost forgotten her father didn't know about them. She never talked about Pastor Landi in front of her father, but she had stopped worrying about what would happen if he found out, since it had been going on so long. But while Leda and her mother had got used to Landi's weekly visits, her father still had heard nothing about them all winter. Then one day in early March, soon after Landi had left Leda's house, her father came storming in, banging the door.

"What's this about you having a young man back to the house, Enkeleda? Don't try and deny it, I've just met the man and he admits it. He says he's been giving you Bible lessons!"

Leda was terrified, but she knew she couldn't get out of admitting it.

"Yes, Babi. He's been teaching me about the Bible. He's a very nice man…"

"Do you know what people will say about me, with my only daughter meeting men behind my back?"

"It wasn't like that, dear," said Leda's mother, nervously. "I was here all the time. They were never alone together. The pastor was just giving Leda lessons to help her education. I didn't see the harm."

"You didn't see the harm?" he shouted. "But you didn't bother to tell me, did you? I thought Beni was making it up when he said Enkeleda was seeing someone, but it seems like the whole village knows and I'm the only one who was kept in the dark." Looking round, he caught sight of Leda's brightly coloured Bible.

"That's the Bible he gave you, is it?" he asked.

"Yes, Babi," said Leda. Her father marched over, picked it up and tried to tear it in half, but it was too thick so he gave up and started ripping handfuls of pages out instead.

When he had finished, and the whole Bible lay in a snowdrift of crumpled pages on the floor, he seemed to calm down a bit.

"This religion stuff brings nothing but trouble. I don't want you to have anything more to do with it. And I'll be taking measures to make sure you don't get into any more trouble!" He didn't say what those measures might be, and Leda didn't dare to ask. Her mother brought over bowls of stew for dinner, and they all ate a very silent meal.

Leda thought and worried about what her father would do to stop her getting into trouble, by which he meant having anything to do with Christians any more. She didn't see what else he could do, since she was already forbidden to go out alone. Maybe he would stop her friends from visiting her, too? Or maybe he would send her to stay with relatives in a more remote village that didn't have a Bible study. But none of her guesses was right. She found out what her father's real plan was early the next week.

On that day her father came home from work early, bringing another man with him that Leda didn't recognise. She stood up, and went to greet the guest.

"Leda, this is Vladimir Gjoni. He lives in the next village, and he owns the petrol station on the main road."

Leda had heard of Mr Gjoni, even though she had never met him. He was meant to be very rich. She put out her hand to shake Mr Gjoni's hand, and was surprised when he kissed her on both cheeks. That wasn't the normal thing for a middle-aged man to do with a young girl he had never met before! Leda looked at her father in confusion, but he avoided her eyes. She looked back at Mr Gjoni, who could see that she was confused.

"You haven't told her?" he boomed cheerfully. "You sly old fox!"

Whatever it was that her father hadn't told her, it seemed to Leda that Mr Gjoni found it very amusing. His fat cheeks wobbled as he laughed and his head, which was mainly bald, turned red. When he had finished laughing he turned to Leda and said,

"Enkeleda, your father has agreed to give you to me as my wife! Now, don't be too shocked," he said, because Leda's mouth had dropped right open, "I may be older than you, but I'm a very wealthy man. My wife will be able to live in luxury! I'm having a new villa built down on the main road, what do you think about that?"

Leda could only manage a sort of "mmm" noise, which sounded like she might be impressed but which actually meant that her head was spinning and she couldn't think of any words. Married? To a man who must be at least forty years old, and probably more? What could her father be thinking of, and why had nobody told her? She was so stunned by the sudden news that she just stood there like an idiot, and her father had to tell her to go and get a drink for Mr Gjoni. As she poured some strong *raki* into two tiny glasses, she noticed that her hand was shaking.

Over on the couch, Leda's father and Mr Gjoni were talking quite cheerfully about what Leda was like and what arrangements they would make for the wedding, as if she wasn't there. Leda supposed she shouldn't find that surprising – after all, they had decided who she was going to marry as if it had nothing to do with her! She knew that some girls, and even some boys, had their marriage arranged for them by their parents, and obviously your parents were allowed to say no if you wanted to marry someone they didn't like, but she had never thought that it would happen like this. She knew her father was angry with her about the Bible lessons, but she had never imagined that she would suddenly find out that he had engaged her to someone she had never met and, as far as she could tell from the five minutes he had been there, someone she didn't even like! As soon as she had given the men the traditional home-made alcoholic drink, *raki*, and some sweets, she went straight back to the kitchen to make the coffee, to avoid having to be near her new "fiancé", but once she had finished making it she had no excuse not to sit on the sofa and start getting to know her future husband.

Once they started talking, it became obvious why her father had chosen this particular man. He asked Leda what she liked to do, if she had any hobbies and so on. Leda supposed that what she should say were things like knitting and crochet, to make herself look like she would be a good wife. But to find out what his attitude was to her belief in God, she took a deep breath and told him that she liked reading the Bible.

"The Bible?" he laughed. "Load of superstitious nonsense! I've never read any of it, and I never intend to. All this religion is just a way for priests to get control over people, but I'm not the kind of man who can be controlled, oh no!" He laughed a bit more at how silly Leda was, and then said, "But if you like reading, don't you worry. We'll get you stacks of magazines. Don't you worry about the expense!" He patted her knee in a patronising way, which made Leda squirm.

Leda was pretty sure now what kind of man Mr Gjoni was. Her father had obviously offered Leda to him as his wife because he would keep her safely away from Christianity and other "nonsense". But she had to make sure, since her whole future life depended on it, so she screwed up her courage and asked, "But, Mr Gjoni, what if I want to keep reading the Bible? And what if I want to go to Bible study or church?"

Mr Gjoni looked at her more seriously.

"No, Enkeleda. You are my fiancée now, and you will not

embarrass me by getting mixed up in religion. Your father told me that you have been going through a childish obsession, and I don't hold that against you because you're very young. But it stops now. My wife will do what I tell her." Then, brightening up, he said, "But you don't have to call me Mr Gjoni! You're going to be my wife! Call me Vladimir."

"Yes, Vladimir," said Leda, trying to smile.

They chatted a little bit more, and then Leda's father suggested that he and Mr Gjoni go out for a drink to celebrate. Leda was not invited. The men left, and Leda was alone. She didn't know where her mother was – it was unusual for her to stay out for so long – but she was glad she was alone so she could think. She tried to imagine what life would be like as Mr Gjoni's – as Vladimir's – wife. She thought about spending every evening with him. He was rich, but she didn't see how piles of magazines, good food and a big TV could make it bearable to live with an ugly, sleazy old man. He sounded as if he would be as bad as her father – "My wife will do what I tell her!" And he wouldn't let her go to Bible study or read the Bible. He would be as bad as her father, but worse, because she would be married to him and could never get away! The future she imagined was horrible, and her dreams of Bible college would disappear. But what choice did she have? She stopped imagining her horrible future and started thinking seriously. *Did* she have a choice?

Leda's mother came in then, distracting her.

"I met your father on the way here – he told me what he's done. Oh, Leda!" She rushed over to the sofa and hugged her daughter. "When he told me to go and see how my mother was doing, I knew he was up to something, but what could I do?"

"How is granny?" asked Leda, distractedly.

"Oh, Leda!" said her mother again, and started crying. Her mother's reaction didn't reassure Leda that this marriage would be a good thing. She decided that she had better start trying to find out a bit more about Mr Gjoni.

Chapter 11

It wasn't easy for Leda to find out much about anything. She was so cut off in the house. She asked her mother a bit about him, but Mami didn't really know him, she had just heard about him. He was very rich, she said, hoping that would cheer Leda up. Leda wanted to know how he had become so rich. Her mother knew he had a petrol station, and thought that must be the reason. But when Leda asked her friend Elona about Mr Gjoni, the next time she came round, she had another answer.

"Yes, he has a petrol station, but haven't you heard about the pyramid scheme?"

"No," said Leda, puzzled. "What's a pyramid scheme?"

"There's a special company," Elona explained. "It's a bit like a bank, but better. You put money in and they give you it back with lots of interest – you can get back twice or three times what you put in, or even more! And you don't have to do anything, you just put the money in and wait."

"That sounds wonderful!" said Leda. "Why doesn't everybody do it?"

"Everybody is!" said Elona. "To tell you a secret..." She leaned forward, her over-long hair falling on Leda's shoulder, and whispered: "My father has sold all his land, and his sheep, and he's putting all the money into the scheme. He says in a few months he'll be able to buy it all back, and have loads of money left over!"

"But is it safe?" said Leda. "How does it work?"

"It must be safe, or people wouldn't be doing it," replied her friend. "And just look at Mr Gjoni – he's made piles! He put his money in right at the beginning, and took it out again when he got the interest. But soon everyone will be nearly as rich as Mr Gjoni, you'll see!"

Leda wasn't sure what to think about the money-making pyramid scheme. If it was true, then it sounded great, but how could it could it work? Where would all the money come from? She asked her mother about it, but she didn't find out much.

"I don't know about that sort of thing, dear. I've heard about it, and I know lots of people are putting their money into it, but I don't know how these things work. One thing I do know, we haven't got any spare money to put in, even if it was paid back a hundred times!"

Leda sighed. When her mother said things like that she felt as if she ought to marry Mr Gjoni, since he had so much money. But could she really give up Jesus, even to make her family rich? She wished she could talk it all over with Suela, but there was still no word. She phoned Suela's parents and got her uncle's number in Tepelena. She tried calling two or three times, but every time someone else would answer the phone and tell her that Suela was fine, but she was busy just now. Each time Leda asked them to leave a message for Suela to call her, but she never got a call back. She hoped nothing was wrong. It wasn't like Suela to ignore her like this.

In the meantime, since she had no other way of finding things out, Leda watched the TV to find out about the pyramid scheme, and anything else that was happening in the world. She tried asking Mr Gjoni about the scheme the next time he came round to visit her for quarter of an hour, as he usually did before going out for drinks with her father for two hours. He chuckled at how clever he had been to get into the scheme early, and said with a sly wink, "I wouldn't like to get into it now!", but that mysterious comment was all he would say on the subject. He didn't think money was a suitable subject for a girl, and said so, so Leda was stuck with trying to find things out from the TV. At least the TV didn't care that she was only a girl! And she had plenty of time to watch it with no Suela, no school and no Bible lessons.

At first there was hardly any mention of the pyramid scheme, except sometimes a comment on how many people had put their money into it. From these comments it sounded as if most of Albania had invested in the money-making scheme. Leda picked up only hints about how it worked – no-one seemed to care very much, as long as they got rich. But then one afternoon a few days later, she turned on the TV to find nothing but the pyramid scheme on all the Albanian channels – but this time it wasn't good news. Something had gone badly wrong. People weren't going to get lots of interest – in fact they weren't even going to get back the money they had put in. They were going to lose everything! Leda watched with her mouth open as the reporters interviewed politicians and money experts, police, and people who had lost money. There were reports of riots starting in towns where people had lost everything – even the houses they lived in. Leda heard the door open and ran towards her mother.

"Mami, the pyramid thing has collapsed! The news says everyone has lost their money!"

"I know!" said Leda's mother. "I just ran into Viola, your friend Elona's mother. She says they had put all their property into the scheme. She's been trying to find out what's going on, but the company isn't answering the phone. She's afraid she's lost everything!" Leda looked at her mother, horrified. Elona's family might have lost everything they had, and they weren't the only ones in the village. How many people had lost out in Albania? How many people wouldn't even have money to buy bread? The fear in Leda's face was reflected in her mother's. What would happen to a country where so many people had lost everything?

The village was buzzing with activity that evening as people went to their neighbours' houses to talk about the crisis. Many women were in tears. The men who had lost everything had empty, shocked faces. A lot of men got drunk and Leda could hear the noise as they passed her house. She and her mother watched the news even though it was just the same things over and over again. When the door opened, they both jumped, but it was just Leda's father and Mr Gjoni. They both seemed to be in a good mood, despite the awful things happening. Leda and her mother got up to greet them, and then started putting things on a tray to serve the guests.

"We have run out of coffee, Leda," her mother said as she poured the drinks. "Nip over to the shop and get some, there's a good girl."

Leda didn't argue. She didn't like spending time with Mr Gjoni, and now it looked as if he was feeling smug because he hadn't lost his money, which made her like him even less. She didn't put on a coat, since it was getting warmer even in the evenings; she just slipped out the door with the money her mother had given her in her hand.

The old lady who ran the shop was pleased to see her. "Leda, there you are! I've been waiting for you to come since yesterday. A certain person dropped off a secret parcel for you!" The old lady winked and smiled so much that it wouldn't have been a secret for long if there had been anyone else around.

"What is it?" asked Leda

"Here it is," said the old lady. "Looks like a book. Does that give you a clue?" She didn't seem to want to give Leda the little newspaper-wrapped parcel, she was enjoying the suspense so much, but Leda waited patiently until the old lady got bored and put it into her hand.

"And a packet of coffee, please," said Leda, putting the note down on the shelf. While the lady went to get it, Leda peeked into the newspaper carefully, not opening it all the way in case it really was something secret. It was a small black book. She pushed the newspaper back a bit further and saw the word "Bible". The pastor! He must have left this here for her. Someone must have told him what happened to her last one. This tiny black book would be easy to hide, not like the big multi-coloured ones that were given out free. He must have bought this for her specially. Leda carefully lifted the cover and read the words "You are never alone, Leda. You are always with Jesus, and everywhere you go you will find your brothers and sisters. I hope this Bible is easier to hide than the last one! God bless you, from Pastor Landi." Leda was really touched, but then the old lady came back with the coffee and her change, so she shut the little book and wrapped it back up in its newspaper. She thanked the old lady for the coffee and the parcel, and went back to the house.

Chapter 12

As she entered the yard with the Bible, Leda suddenly thought, *I can't go into the house with this parcel! They will see it, and ask me what it is, and that will be the end of that!* She thought quickly, and had an idea. She took the packet of coffee out of the plastic bag, put the parcel into it, and hid it under the chickens' water bowl. She looked around – no-one had seen her. It was beginning to get dark, anyway. She walked into the house, hoping her mother wouldn't ask her why she hadn't got a bag for the coffee, but she was busy knitting on the sofa, and didn't say anything. Leda made the coffee with a secret smile on her face. What would Babi and Mr Gjoni say if they knew the secret that came with their coffee? She managed to wipe the smirk off her face as she went to serve the men the steaming drinks.

Leda's father and Mr Gjoni were talking about the pyramid scheme collapsing, just like everyone else in the village. But unlike the other people in the village, and the angry, shouting people on the TV, Babi and Mr Gjoni didn't seem upset at all. In fact, Mr Gjoni seemed rather pleased. He was explaining to Leda's parents why he had taken his money out of the scheme earlier.

"It's always useful to have a few friends in the government, you see. So, this chap I know, he told me that the scheme was dodgy, that it might all go down the plughole. Just between us, of course – he could have lost his job over it. I suppose I could have realised for myself; I mean, nothing that good can last for long, right?"

Leda's father nodded, as if he understood all about complicated investments.

"So, of course, it turned out he was right. It happened a bit later than he thought, and I could have made more if I'd kept my money in longer, but on the whole I've done pretty well. I just pity those poor fools who poured all their money in with blind trust. They don't understand capitalism, that's the trouble. Well, they're learning now!" Mr Gjoni laughed, and Leda's father joined in. It was clear that Mr Gjoni didn't pity the people who had lost their money; he just thought they were stupid. She thought of Elona's family, who had lost everything, and it made her hot and angry to see Mr Gjoni laughing at them. And her father, too, who hadn't lost any money only because he hadn't had any to put into the scheme! Leda sat very still and didn't say anything so the men wouldn't see how angry she was.

Mr Gjoni finally noticed his fiancée.

"You're very quiet tonight, Leda!" he said, rubbing her knee. "What's the matter? Are you frightened by all of those riots on the TV?"

Leda shrugged. "I suppose so," she said.

"Oh, don't you worry about them, sweetheart. There won't be anything like that in this little village. But don't go out tonight, just to be safe. There are a lot of angry people." He turned to Leda's father. "Actually, we would be better to go to my petrol station for a drink tonight. The mood is rough, and the villagers won't be too pleased to see me, since I've still got my money!" He laughed and pulled a big wad of notes out of his pocket. Leda had seen him do this before. He enjoyed showing off this way. But tonight, before he and her father left for their usual drink, he turned towards Leda with the money still in his hand. He plucked off a few notes and handed them to Leda.

"There you go, sweetheart. Buy yourself some nice clothes. You need to get used to the good life, since you're going to be my wife!"

Leda watched the two men go out the door and shut it behind them. Then she looked down at the money in her hand. She counted the notes – one, two, three, four, five. Five thousand lekë. That was more money than she had ever held before, like five years' New Year presents put together. She looked at her mother, expecting her to say she couldn't have it, but Mami just shrugged.

"I suppose you'd better do what he says, if that's what he wants to do with his money. We can go to the market tomorrow."

Leda thought she could buy a whole wardrobe of clothes from the market with this money. In fact, she could probably afford to buy clothes from the shops in the city! But she had other plans for the money. An idea was growing at the back of her mind.

That night, Leda couldn't sleep. Lying awake reminded her of the night Geni left, more than half a year ago. She was a lot more used to praying now than she had been that night. She slipped out of bed, knelt down and closed her eyes.

"Father God," she began. "You know why I'm praying to

you just now. You know what I'm thinking of doing. Yesterday morning I didn't have anything. Now I have a Bible and money, there's chaos everywhere, and I have the chance to get away and not get caught. I know I'm supposed to obey my parents, but if I obey my father then I'll have to marry a man who won't let me obey you!" Leda sighed. "Lord, I'm confused about what's the right thing to do. Please let me know if I should do it."

She waited in the dark, not knowing what exactly to expect. She was stressed and tense, but slowly she felt peace sweep over her like a gentle wave. She knew it was from Jesus. And she knew what she had to do.

Getting to her feet, she took a plastic bag and put in some a few spare clothes, some bread and an apple. She got dressed and put on her jacket. She picked the five bank notes off the table and shoved them deep in her pocket. Then she crept towards the door. She knew that her father had come in drunk and wouldn't hear anything, but her mother might. She eased the door open as slowly as she could, slipped out, and drew it closed after her. Outside it was chilly and quiet. The chickens were asleep in their little shelter. She crept up to their water bowl, lifted it, and saw that her secret Bible was still safe. She took it out of the plastic bag, which was now dirty, and put it into the bag with her clothes. Then she crept out of the yard, lifting the gate on its hinges as she turned it, so it wouldn't squeal, and started the journey that she knew would be the longest and scariest of her life.

Chapter 13

It was a long walk down to the main road from the village. Leda couldn't get lost, as she just had to keep following the road down, but she could trip over stones, and slip in mud, and get caught by branches, and stumble into streams in the dark, and she managed to do all of those things, lots of times. She wished she had a torch, or that the moon was brighter and didn't keep going behind clouds. She fell a couple of times, and once she lost her bag, but the bright plastic was easy to see even by moonlight so she found it again. She checked quickly whether she could feel the newspaper, so she would know the Bible was still there, and then she set off again. She couldn't afford to dawdle. She had to be down to the main road in time to catch a really early minibus so that she would be far away before anyone knew she was gone. If someone came after her in a car before she had managed to board a minibus, they would catch up with her in no time!

When she wasn't too busy tripping over, Leda thought that maybe she was lucky it was such hard going. It kept her warm in the chilly night, and it stopped her mind from wandering and thinking about wolves. It was March, not midwinter, so the wolves shouldn't be starving, and Leda knew that wolves only attacked humans when they were starving – but still, she was glad she didn't have too much time to worry about the fierce creatures that could be watching her.

After a while, Leda found that the going was easier. She wasn't tripping as much, or getting as out of breath. She had been keeping her eyes fixed on the path, so she hadn't noticed the gradual change, but when she looked up she noticed that the sky was turning lighter, and she was on flatter ground – and she could see the main road in the distance! The sight gave her a new burst of energy, and by the time the sun was peeping between the gaps in the mountains, Leda had arrived at the main road. There was no traffic on the road. She crossed to the other side, where the minibuses would be going south, and put her bag on the ground.

Leda had never travelled alone, and hadn't been out of her own village for years. She was very nervous. She shivered as she waited, although the day was warming up. A car passed her. It slowed down to see if she wanted a lift, but she was scared to take a lift on her own with a man she didn't know. She hoped travelling by minibus would be safe. It was very early and no other vehicles came along for a while. Then she heard an engine and looked up. It was a minibus! She was just putting her hand out to signal for it when she noticed the registration plate. It had "MK" for Mallakaster at the beginning – it was from the local area. It could be someone who knew her! Quickly, she turned away and walked further down the road, trying to turn her face away as much as possible without looking suspicious. She heard the minibus slow down, and she was terrified it was going to stop anyway, but then she heard it carry on, and when she turned around she found it had slowed down to turn up the road to the mountain villages – the same road she had come down.

Still shaking from the mistake she had nearly made, Leda watched another car go past, and then later a couple of cars and a lorry. She had another half hour to wait, and had finished her packed breakfast before the next minibus came along. It had registration plates from the city of Fier. That was far enough away, so Leda took a deep breath and signalled with her hand. The minibus slowed down and pulled over next to her. Another passenger slid the door open for her and Leda got in.

"Where are you going?" the driver asked. Leda hadn't actually decided. She couldn't just say "Away from my fiancé!", so she thought for a second and then said "Tepelena." That was where Suela was. Maybe she would know what Leda should do next. The driver pulled out, and the minibus set off along the windy, bumpy road to Tepelena with Leda in it.

After only a minute or so they passed a petrol station that Leda knew must be the one that Vladimir Gjoni owned. It was big and new-looking, but even though she had never seen it before, Leda was glad she was seeing the back of it. For a horrible moment she wondered if the driver would pull in for fuel and Mr Gjoni might see her, but the minibus trundled past without pausing. Leda was next to the window and as they rolled and bumped along she watched the scenery they passed, bits of Albania she had never seen and might never have seen if she had stayed in the village and married Mr Gjoni. The minibus climbed up high into the mountains, onto a windy, narrow road with nothing on the right hand side but a steep drop down to the valley. Leda could see the twisty road for a long way ahead; then it would disappear as they went round another tight bend, and appear again in a few seconds after another bend. The mountains stretched out to the right, looking smaller since the bus was on high ground. It looked as if there were no people for miles, but Leda knew that out there in the mountains there were probably lots of villages like hers, full of girls like her who had never known any other kind of life. So what was she doing here, on the road to somewhere she had never been before, with no plan?

She had been lost in looking at the mountains and didn't notice the minibus slowing down until they pulled in to a parking area at the side of the road. Leda suddenly felt panicked.

"What's going on? Why have we stopped?" she asked, trying not to sound to frightened.

A middle-aged lady sitting next to her replied, "We've just stopped for breakfast. I've been on this minibus since Fier! I need a coffee." Leda slipped out of the minibus. It was nice to be on her feet again. Her bottom had started to hurt in the old, uncomfortable minibus on the bumpy roads. She was still a bit hungry, actually, and with all that money in her pocket she could afford to buy herself something. She trooped into the café with the other passengers and ordered a bowl of yoghurt and a peach juice. Then she saw something that almost took away her appetite. The café had a TV up in the corner of the room, and it was showing scenes of rioting from yesterday, but underneath that, the breaking news came up in headlines. It said something about guns. Leda went over to read the details in the smaller print. It said that crowds had broken into the military arsenals, the places where the army kept all their guns and weapons. People angry about losing all their money now had loads of guns! Leda felt cold. She didn't remember ever feeling in so much danger. It seemed as if her whole country had turned into a danger zone. When her food arrived she spooned it into her mouth without tasting it, her eyes on the TV.

Everyone else had seen the news, too, and when they got back into the minibus after a quarter of an hour, some of the passengers asked the driver to tune the radio to the news. What they heard wasn't reassuring. In some towns people had taken the weapons and invaded the police stations. The police had nothing to do with the problem, but they were connected to the government, so they would do. The news said there were no police to be found – they had just taken off their uniforms and hidden. Now there was no police force and angry people with stolen guns were in charge! Leda felt like crying. The lady next to her saw her face and put an arm around her, rubbing her shoulder. Eventually the driver put the radio back on the music because they had heard all of the news and it was just repeating itself. Leda was glad not to hear the horrible news any more.

They had gradually been coming down from the mountains, and the road had been getting less twisty. Suddenly Leda noticed lots of buildings coming up – a town. She leaned forward in her seat.

"Is this Tepelena? I'm going to Tepelena!" she shouted over the radio. The driver just laughed.

"This? This is just Memaliaj. It's not even a proper town, just a tiny place. You'll be in Tepelena in about ten minutes, and you'll know when you get there!"

No-one had to get on or off at Memaliaj, so Leda just saw a glimpse of it as they sailed through. She saw a long street stretching right down the hill to an enormous river with a ferry crossing. If this place, so much bigger than her village, wasn't even a proper town, what on earth was Tepelena like?

She found out soon enough, as the driver had said. They

travelled for a few more minutes, then turned a corner and started going downhill. Then Leda could see Tepelena ahead of her. Ahead of them were big factory buildings and warehouses, and directly above those, towering on a high cliff, was the town itself, full of tall blocks of flats. The town disappeared from view for a while as they travelled along the side of the cliff, but suddenly they emerged into a big, open space, where they came to a stop. Leda saw cafés and travel agents all around, a big hotel and even a statue of a man who looked like a Turk, smoking a pipe and staring towards the mountain opposite. All the way towards the cliff edge the town stretched, and away up the hill she could see a war memorial. This place was huge! How on earth would she find Suela here? She noticed that the driver was talking to her.

"It's two hundred *lekë*."

Leda had some change from the restaurant, so she gave him two hundred and got out of the minibus. The minibus set off again, and she stood in Tepelena all alone, her one little plastic bag in her hand, wondering what to do next.

Chapter 14

She decided to head into town to see if she could find a phone box to call Suela's uncle. He might just say Suela was out like he always did, but surely if she told them she was in Tepelena he would let her come and wait at the house? But what if he wondered why she was in Tepelena, and phoned Suela's parents to check everything was ok? Leda wandered slowly in search of a phone box, not sure whether it was a good idea or not, when suddenly she heard someone talking loudly in a foreign language. She looked round and saw a tall young man with expensive clothes and sunglasses talking loudly into a mobile phone. Leda had heard of mobile phones but she had never seen one before. She wondered how they worked. Without realising it, she took a few steps towards the young man. He didn't notice, he was too busy going on and on in the language that Leda now realised was Italian.

Someone else had noticed her, though. Leda's attention was drawn by someone waving their arms inside the café in front of her. It was a pretty girl of about her own age with long, dangly earrings, a tight top and lots of makeup. Leda wondered who the girl was waving to when she suddenly realised it was Suela!

Ignoring the man speaking Italian, she rushed inside and hugged her friend.

"Suela! How are you? Why did you never call me back?"

"Leda! What on earth are you doing here? Does your father know you're here? Did you come to find me?"

They breathlessly asked each other questions for the first minute, then calmed down enough to start telling each other the answers. Suela wasn't surprised Leda had run away.

"My mami told me you were engaged to Vladimir Gjoni! I couldn't believe it when I heard. I would have run away, too!"

"Why didn't you call me back? I would have told you all about it myself!"

"Did you call me? I wondered why you hadn't ever called. No one told me, it feels like everyone's keeping secrets from me! I was going to call you, I really wanted to, but I wasn't allowed to call anyone except my parents."

Leda was about to ask what she meant by "not allowed" when the Italian-speaker came in. All of a sudden, Suela calmed down and became very cool.

"Hi, Maks," she said. "This is a friend of mine from home. She's passing through Tepelena today. I thought I might take her to the café with the nice view, since you're so busy with all this visa business."

"Hi," said Maks to Leda, shaking her hand. "Nice to meet you." Turning to Suela, he said,

"Yeah, why not? I'm up to my ears with all this visa hassle. It wouldn't be worth it if it wasn't for such a lovely girl!"

He smiled at Suela, and she smiled back, but Leda knew her friend well enough to know that it was a forced smile. Something was wrong between Suela and her tall, handsome fiancé.

The two girls picked up their jackets while Maks paid the bill. Then they all walked casually along the square towards the road out of Tepelena. Maks didn't know that Leda had run away from home, and there was definitely something Suela hadn't told Leda yet, and even Maks himself seemed shifty as if he had a secret, but they all tried to act perfectly natural as they strolled along. Maks walked them all the way to the café Suela had talked about, which was about five minutes out of town. Then he gave Suela a bit of money to pay for their drinks, and went back towards town, saying he had to deal with the "visa business".

The girls climbed up to the top floor of the café and sat down. Leda was amazed by the view of the mountain valley below, with a slow river winding along pure white stone. She thought it was the most beautiful valley she had ever seen, but she wasn't able to look at it long because Suela grabbed her hand and started speaking urgently in a low voice.

"Leda, listen to me. I was wrong about Maks. He's trying to get a fiancée visa to take me to Italy, and he says he's going to marry me there, but I know he's not! He thinks I don't know Italian, but I learnt it from watching all those Italian films they show on TV." Leda nodded. She knew plenty of people who had learnt Italian or Greek from TV programmes.

"Well, because he doesn't know I speak Italian, he talks to his business partners in Italy when I can hear. Leda, he doesn't want to marry me. He's planning to get me out of the country and then sell me to someone he knows. I heard them agreeing the price. Leda, he's going to sell me as a slave!"

"Are you sure?" Leda asked, her face going pale with shock.

"I'm absolutely sure! He's even arranged where he's going to meet his friend to pass me on to him. He says he'll tell me we're going to take a holiday to look for good places to go on honeymoon, and then he'll tell my family I ran off with someone else while we were travelling."

The desperation on Suela's face convinced Leda, even though she didn't want to believe something so horrible could be true.

"That would certainly explain why Maks wanted such a sudden engagement," she said.

The waiter came and brought them their drinks, which gave Suela a chance to calm down and Leda a chance to think. When he had gone she asked, "Why don't you tell your parents or your uncle?"

"Maks is always there when I phone my parents, and he won't let me phone anyone else. I'm afraid of what he would do if I told anyone. I think my uncle is afraid of him, too. He controls everything, Leda – he even tells me what to wear! I think he has a gun. I'm really scared of him!" Suela started to cry. Leda handed her a napkin and pulled her chair round so that she could to put an arm round her.

"When do you think he will get the visa?" she asked.

"I don't know," said Suela, blowing her nose. "He was supposed to have it by now, because he bribed someone, but all this chaos with the pyramid scheme is holding things up. But he's been shouting into that phone all day – I'm sure he'll get results soon."

"Then we need to move even sooner, don't we?" said Leda.

Suela nodded. The girls could see they were both thinking along the same lines. They got up and paid the waiter on the way out. Then, instead of turning back towards Tepelena, they turned the other way and started walking down the road that led further south.

"I'm sorry we can't go back and get your stuff," Leda said as they walked along. "But this is the best chance we've got. We can get a minibus without Maks finding out."

"But Leda," said Suela, "I've got hardly any money. Maks makes sure he never gives me more than the price of a couple of drinks. I don't think I've got enough for both of us on a minibus." Leda smiled and pulled the roll of money out of her pocket so that just the top showed.

"Mr Gjoni has paid our fares!" she said. Both girls laughed, but suddenly they heard something that stopped them dead. Gunfire! And coming this way, fast! They both threw themselves down at the side of the road as a car hurtled past, the passenger letting off bursts of gunfire through the sunroof as they went. The car whizzed round the next bend, out of sight, and the two girls picked themselves up.

"It's been like that all day here," said Suela. "And it's only going to get worse. Leda, since we're running away anyway, maybe we should run *all* the way. Albania's going crazy just now. Why don't we go over the mountains, to Greece?"

Chapter 15

Leda looked at Suela. She could see she was serious, but could it be done? Girls never went over the mountains, only strong boys. Would they actually get there, or would they get lost, or stuck on the mountains? She didn't have much time to think because a minibus was coming down the road, and Suela had her hand out.

"Please, Leda!" said Suela, as she signalled for the driver to stop. "I've got a cousin in Gjirokaster. He can show us the way, or find us someone who can. Do you really think it's more dangerous to try and make it over the mountains than to stay here and get shot, or sold, or married to Mr Gjoni?" The minibus had stopped and the door was opening. Suela was begging Leda with her eyes.

"Okay!" said Leda, her mind suddenly made up. She climbed into the minibus and gave Suela a hand inside. They were thrown back in their seats as the minibus pulled out sharply. Leda looked at Suela, and Suela looked back. They were both scared, but they were together, and they had a chance! Leda took Suela's hand and squeezed it as the minibus sped south to the city of Gjirokaster.

There was almost an hour of twisty, cliff-edge road between

Tepelena and Gjirokaster. Suela had been taken to Gjirokaster a couple of times by her uncle, so she knew the road, but to Leda it was all new. It was a beautiful area but a dangerous road. The driver, obviously used to the route, drove as if there was no cliff edge next to him and no chance of falling. Leda prayed silently as they drove along that they would be okay. It didn't seem safe to talk about their plans in a crowded minibus, so she and Suela chatted about what they had both been up to since they had last seen each other. Leda told Suela the story of her father tearing up her Bible, and the pastor secretly giving her a new one. Suela told Leda about how she had spent her time over the summer going fishing with her cousins at the river.

"It was so boring, but this one time when Damo finally caught a fish, he slipped on the rock and it pulled him in!"

Leda shivered in sympathy. The local spring was called "Cold Water", and Suela had told her it deserved its name. The ride passed quickly as they chatted, and Leda found that a lot of the things that had happened to her seemed a lot funnier and less scary now that she had Suela to share them with. Suela chattered and giggled on and on, and Leda started to enjoy herself, despite being on the run. She didn't notice that they had arrived until the minibus stopped and people started getting out. Suela looked round.

"Oh," she exclaimed. "This is Gjirokaster. Quick, let's get out." Leda leaned forward to pay the driver, waited for her change, and then followed Suela out of the minibus. It was midday by now, and Leda's stomach was starting to rumble.

"I could do with some lunch," she said, plaintively. Suela smiled.

"I know the perfect place." She put her arm through Suela's and led her towards the city centre.

They had been down on the main road where the buses and minibuses stopped, and Leda hadn't seen the town itself, but as Suela led her along and they turned up the main street into the town, the size of the place took her breath away. It must have been three or four times the size of Tepelena! The broad main street went up and up for what looked like miles. Leda thought she could see a big market much further up the hill, but she wasn't sure at this distance. What she was sure of was the huge castle looming over the town. This was *argiro kastro*, the "silver castle" Gjirokaster was named for, and it was enormous. Leda had never seen a castle before. She had never seen any building so big except in films. She squinted against the sun to see it more clearly, but Suela was pulling her along.

"Don't stare, people will start to notice you. And anyway, I'm dying for lunch. Come on."

"It's so big! It's even bigger than Tepelena, much bigger!"

"Of course it is, Tepelena's just a little town," replied her friend casually, as if she hadn't spent her life in the same tiny village as Leda. "Now please, come *on*!"

The two girls tramped up the hill, past the vandalised police station with no sign of police, and past buildings with bullet holes in them and broken windows. In the daylight it didn't look so scary, but Leda could imagine that it must have been terrifying last night, with so much shooting going on. She hoped they wouldn't be staying in Gjirokaster tonight. After a tiring walk that took them less than halfway up the huge hill, they came to the pizza restaurant, Suela's favourite. They went in and took their seats in a corner so that not too many people would see them. There wasn't much chance they would be recognised, but it was better to be careful. The pizza was great. It was the first Leda had ever tried, although Suela was obviously an expert. As they were relaxing afterwards with full stomachs, an important thought suddenly occurred to Leda.

"Suela, your shoes! You can't go hill-walking in those!" Suela looked down at her feet. She was wearing bright pink pointy-toed, high-heeled shoes.

"Oh no!" she said. "You're right. Maks always said I had to dress 'like a proper bride-to-be'. My trainers are back in Tepelena. What are we going to do?"

"It's alright," said Leda. "We can use some of Mr Gjoni's money. As long as we get them from the market, we can afford them." She looked at her watch. "But it's after one o'clock! The market will be closing soon. Come on, we'd better hurry."

They rushed out of the restaurant and up the hill towards the market. The hill seemed even steeper now that they were in a hurry. When they got to the market most stalls were still open, although a few were packing up. The stalls selling shoes were right up the top, so they had to push their way past people trying to buy or sell jeans and tops, wool and thread, jewellery, hair clips, clothes brushes, plastic carpet sweepers, tobacco, watches, and all sorts of other things they weren't looking for. Suela soon found a sturdy-looking pair of trainers. They used up over a thousand *lekë* paying for them and the socks Suela needed to go with them. Then Suela persuaded Leda that they should get a cheap rucksack, too, since carrying a plastic bag would be difficult when climbing the mountain, and the plastic might tear. Leda looked at the cash they had left – only half of what she had started out with. She pushed it back into her pocket and hoped it would be enough to take them to the end of their journey, wherever that might be.

Chapter 16

With her new trainers on her feet and her pink shoes in the new rucksack along with Leda's clothes, Suela set out to find her cousin. He lived in area called "18th of September", a little further down the hill they had just come up. As they turned off the main road and entered the crowded neighbourhood, full of identical blocks of flats and muddy streets with no names, Leda wondered how on earth they would find Suela's cousin's house, but her friend didn't seem to have any difficulty. Soon they were standing outside a block of flats which looked just like all the others, and Suela was giving Leda instructions.

"I can't go up because if anyone else answers the door they'll know who I am, and they'll tell my uncle in Tepelena. Maks would come and get us!"

"But I don't even know what your cousin looks like!" protested Leda.

"Just ask for Laert. If he's in, tell him someone wants to speak to him downstairs. If not, find out where he is!"

Leda climbed the stairs to the fourth floor, where Laert's family lived, and knocked. The door was opened by a girl of about twelve.

"Is Laert in?" Leda asked.

"No, sorry, he's out playing pool. He'll be in at teatime."

It looked as if she was about to shut the door, so Leda asked quickly, "Where does he play pool? I don't know this neighbourhood very well."

"It's just round the corner," the girl said. "Next to the butcher's. You'll find it easily."

Leda came back down, and she and Suela set off to find the pool club. It wasn't as easy to find as all that, but after a bit of asking around they found the place. It was smoky inside, and full of strange men. Both girls were a bit afraid to go in alone, so they went in together. Suela spotted Laert and went over to him. She explained in a whisper what the situation was, and he replied quietly. Suela came back over to Leda.

"He will help us out. He's got a friend who can take us to Greece tonight. He says to wait for him outside."

They sat outside, doing nothing, for about half an hour. Little kids from the neighbourhood came over to look at them and ask what they were called, but they soon got bored and went off to play elsewhere. Eventually Laert came out. He was in a good mood because he had won, and insisted on taking them for a drink to talk about their plans. The girls were nervous about trusting anyone else with the secret that they were running away, but Laert didn't seem to have a problem with their decision.

"Yeah, I've got a friend who can take you over the mountains. He's been up there loads of times. You give me your money, and I'll see if he's free tonight. You two shouldn't hang around any longer than you need to. That Maks might catch you, and I wouldn't want to be you it he did! Anyway, it's not safe for anyone round here at the moment with all the guns around."

Laert led them through backstreets and across a small park to a poorer neighbourhood, full of stray dogs and junk lying around. He took them to a tiny flat where his friend lived. Inside there were more people than Leda or Suela had ever seen in one little flat, all of them quite dark-skinned. His friend's mother and sister lived there, along with his grandmother, his brother and his sister's small children. There was hardly room to sit down, but the family were very welcoming. They seemed to be used to strange people dropping round, and they brought the girls something to drink while Laert went off to try and find his friend.

Laert took ages. The afternoon wore on, and the girls ended up having tea with the large Gypsy family, who kindly made enough for them, too. Leda was nervous. What if Laert didn't come back tonight, or if his friend wasn't free? It wouldn't take long for Maks to start looking for them, and Gjirokaster was a fairly obvious place to start.

It was starting to get dark when Laert finally did come back, and he had his friend Martin with him, a thin boy of about twenty with sunken cheeks, high cheekbones and the dark skin of the rest of his family.

"Yeah, Martin can take you tonight," Laert said, as soon as he sat down. "Martin, these are the girls I was telling you about."

Laert had a plastic bag in his hand, which he handed to Suela. It contained bottles of water, snacks, and a small torch. Suela put it in the rucksack. Then Laert handed some money to Leda.

"I've paid Martin," he said. "And I've changed the rest into Greek money for you."

Leda looked at the strange notes in her hand. She didn't

know how much drachmas were worth, but she knew there couldn't be much left from the five thousand. She found herself worrying again about what they would do when it ran out, but she told herself to pray, not worry.

It was fully dark now, and a few gunshots had already started ringing out, but they had to wait until Martin had eaten before they could set off. Just as he was finishing, a car tooted outside.

"That will be my friend now," said Martin, wiping his mouth. "He'll give us a lift to near the border."

The girls got up and put on their jackets. Their hearts were hammering. It was really happening! They kissed Martin's relatives goodbye, leaving them Suela's shiny pink shoes as a present, and thanked Laert for all his help. Then they followed Martin out of the house and got into the back of a rickety, very old car.

The car trundled off down the hill and soon they were leaving Gjirokaster behind. The noise and flashes of gunfire gradually died away as they bumped along the quiet, flat stretch that led from Gjirokaster to the Greek border. After about half an hour the car pulled off the road and started to climb up a narrow track through the hills. It was a very dark, twisty road, and sometimes branches scraped against the windows. Suela grabbed Leda's hand, but Leda knew that the scary bit was still to come, when they got out of the car and started the journey on foot. After another twenty minutes or so, Leda saw the lights of a village ahead, and the car stopped at the side of the road. Martin said goodbye to his friend and got out of the car. The girls followed, and stood shivering in the dark as Martin's friend drove away from them down to the village, where there would be room to turn round. Martin didn't wait to see him go. He looked around for a few seconds, found the goat track he was looking for, and started to follow it up the hill. He looked around at the girls.

"Come on!" he hissed. Leda and Suela looked at each other nervously. Leda gave Suela's hand a quick squeeze, and then let go and started to follow Martin up the goat track. Suela followed behind her. By the time Martin's friend had turned his car and driven back up the road past them, they were well above him on the hill. Leda looked back at the taillights of the car below her, driving away and leaving them on the dark hill. Now they were really committed. There was no going back.

Chapter 17

The path wound up the hill, higher and higher. Leda and especially Suela were already out of breath, but Martin was obviously used to these paths and just kept going.

"How long does it take?" asked Leda, after they had climbed for a while.

"About six hours, usually," said Martin quietly.

"Six hours!" gasped Suela. "Is it this steep all the way?"

"Shh!" said Martin fiercely, and the girls shut up. Leda didn't know who Martin thought might hear – the only living creatures they had seen so far were some sleepy sheep. But he was their guide, so it was best to do what he said.

When they reached the crest of the hill there was a flattish walk for a while, which was a relief for the girls, but soon they set off upwards again. Now they were getting into the proper mountains, and the way got rockier and harder. They weren't on a goat track anymore; they were just trusting to Martin's sense of direction. Leda didn't know how he could find the way on such a cloudy night, but she just had to hope that he could. They climbed on and on, stumbling on rocks and roots, scraping their hands on the bits where they had to clamber on all fours. Leda knew that Suela would have been complaining fiercely if Martin hadn't insisted on no noise. When she looked back, Leda could see the tiny lights of villages behind them, but she didn't have much time to look around. Martin kept them climbing as fast as they could go, and even when they were on quite flat bits, or going downhill, still the ground wasn't clear and they had to be very careful all the time.

Leda wasn't sure exactly what time they had set off, but it had to be well past midnight by now. She was hungry again, her feet hurt, her legs hurt, her hands hurt, and she just wanted to sit down for a while. She was thinking of pleading with Martin that they take a break, but before she could, he suggested it himself. The girls threw themselves down gratefully and started to dig out the food Laert had packed for them. It was hard eating in the dark, and when Suela felt the torch in the bag, she thought that it was a good idea to use it. She clicked it on and smiled at Leda, but the smile soon fell away when Martin hissed, "What are you doing?!" and snatched it out of her hand. He turned it off and sat down beside them. "We are really close to the Greek border now. There are border guards. If they see that, we'll get caught. I've been caught by the border guards once before, and it's not something I want to go through again!" Martin shuddered. So did the girls. If the border guards frightened Martin, they must be pretty bad.

All too soon they were setting off again. There was more climbing, more stumbling, more sweating and aching and scrabbling. Every so often Leda and Suela would swap the rucksack over between them. Every so often Martin would signal them to stop. Then he would go on ahead and come back a few minutes later, waving them on again. It seemed like they had been travelling all night, and as if this night had been going on for days and days. Sometimes it felt as if they would be climbing in these mountains forever. But eventually, and without warning, when they were on a downward stretch through a forest, Martin stopped and said, "This is it. This is where I leave you. You're in Greece now. You should stay in this forest for the rest of the night, and creep out at first light. There shouldn't be any border guards then. The road to Ioannina is just on the other side of this wood, just follow the road down." He turned to go.

"Wait!" said Suela. "You can't just leave us like this! We don't know where we are and it's nighttime and we'll be all alone!"

"What do you want me to do?" said Martin. "Hold your hands all the way to Athens? I have to get back to Albania before it gets light!"

Suela still looked upset, but Leda said, "He's right, Suela. And he's risked a lot bringing us here. Thank you, Martin. God protect you on your journey back." Martin shook Leda's hand, and set off back the way he had come. In the darkness of the nighttime forest, he was out of sight before he had taken five steps. The girls were alone.

Leda could hear Suela sniffing and breathing too fast. It was clear she was still frightened and upset.

"Come on, let's sit down," Leda said. We're not going anywhere for a while."

She pulled out the plastic bags their food had been wrapped in, and they sat on them on the hard forest floor. Suela had started crying properly now.

"This was a stupid idea," she sobbed, quietly. "What are we going to do? Where are we going to go? We'll get caught by the border guards, or attacked by wolves or sheepdogs, or get lost and die up here!"

Leda hugged her friend and rocked her. "It will be okay. We've already done the hard bit. We just have to sit it out 'til morning, alright?" Suela didn't seem to cheer up very much, but Leda had a better idea for comforting her. She pulled out her new little Bible, still covered in the newspaper, and the torch. When she switched on the torch, Suela seemed frightened again.

"Leda – you know what Martin said!"

"But that was on top of the mountain, and now we're hidden in the forest. It will be okay. Now listen."

She rifled through the pages looking for the passage she wanted. It wasn't easy when it was a Bible she hadn't used before, and it was doubly difficult doing it with one hand while holding a torch in the other, but eventually she found the bit she was looking for.

"Listen to this, Suela. This is what made me feel better when Geni went over the mountains, when he was in the situation we are now."

And she read, "You will keep in perfect peace him whose mind is steadfast, because his trust is in you. Trust in the Lord forever, for the Lord, the Lord, is the rock eternal. My soul yearns for you in the night; in the morning my spirit longs for you."

"That's beautiful," said Suela, sounding calmer already. "What is it?"

"That's from a book called Isaiah. There are loads of lovely bits in Isaiah, and the rest of the Bible."

"Keep reading to me," said Suela. "I feel much safer when you read those things about God protecting us."

So Leda kept reading. She read Suela other bits from Isaiah, and then some of her favourite psalms:

"Even though I walk through the valley as dark as death I will not be afraid, because you are with me."

She was going to try and find some of the speeches that Jesus had given, when she noticed that Suela was asleep. Leda smiled. That was the best way to get through the wait until dawn. She wondered if she could manage to drift off, too. She sat back against a tree and tried to get comfortable, but it was impossible. The roots were hard under her bottom, the bark was rough against her back, and small branches poked at her from every side. Sure that she wouldn't be able to sleep, Leda decided to pray. She remembered, as Pastor Landi had told her, to thank God for things and not just give him a list of requests. So she thanked God for getting them this far safely, and that Suela had been able to sleep, and that they were now safe from Maks and Mr Gjoni. And then she asked God to take them the rest of the way to somewhere safe, and that Martin would get back home without getting caught, and that Maks wouldn't be able to find any other girls to trap into slavery. By this time Leda was yawning every few seconds. The tree hadn't got any more comfortable, but she had stopped noticing so much. Her head nodded gradually forward, and she fell asleep.

Chapter 18

Leda was woken up by Suela shaking her.

"Leda, Leda, it's light! I don't know how long we've slept. Shouldn't we be going down to the road?"

Leda opened her eyes and shivered. She felt terrible. Her bottom was numb, her back was sore and she had a terrible crick in her neck from sleeping sitting up. But Suela was right, it was daytime, and they had to get moving. She struggled to her feet and stretched to get her arms and legs working again. Suela looked as rough as Leda felt as they stumbled down the hill through the forest. Not far on, the forest came to an end and Leda could see the road Martin had told them about. Between them and the road was an open stretch of hillside, which made Leda nervous, but she couldn't see anybody about so they set off. They only saw two or three cars and a bus go by as they climbed down, but it was still quite early in the morning. The road was clear when they arrived at it. Now they had a dilemma.

"How are we going to travel?" said Suela. "We can't stay here at the border but I don't know where we should be heading for. Maybe we should just get the first bus that comes along?"

Leda looked at the small bunch of drachmas. "I don't know if we've got enough for the bus, and anyway a bus just went past. There might not be one for a while."

"Well what *are* we going to do, then?" said Suela. "We can't just walk all the way to Athens, or Thessaloniki, or wherever!"

"I know, I know," said Leda distractedly, watching the road. She knew of another way, but she wasn't sure what Suela would think of it. Suela guessed it without Leda saying.

"Hitchhiking? You must be mad! It's dangerous, everybody knows that, and they'll realise we're illegal immigrants and take us to the police!"

"I know," said Leda. "But what choice do we have? I really think it's that or walking." Suela still shook her head determinedly. Leda wasn't sure whether she should mention her prayer from last night, wondering if it would make any difference to Suela's opinion, but she thought she should be honest. "Suela, I know it's dangerous, and I know you're scared – so am I. But I was praying last night while you were asleep. I believe that God will look after us; he's helped us this far. I think he cares about us, and he can protect us even here. He'll make this work out for the best, like it says in the Bible."

It took Leda a long time to persuade Suela, and a few cars went by in the meantime. In the end, Suela gave in.

"Alright! But if the person who stops looks dodgy, we're not getting in. Okay?"

"Okay," said Leda.

Leda had seen hitchhikers on films, so she knew that you put your thumb out. She tried this with the next car but it just carried on past without slowing down. The one after that slowed down and stopped just ahead of them. Leda and Suela hurried after it, clutching the rucksack. The man in the car was suntanned, balding and slightly plump. He looked friendly, and he sounded friendly from the way he was talking away to them, but since it was in Greek they didn't understand a word. Leda looked at Suela, who paused and then gave a tiny nod, and they got into the back seat. Leda didn't know any Greek apart from the word for thank you, which she said to the man. She whispered to Suela to ask if she knew any more, but unfortunately she didn't. The man didn't seem bothered that they didn't answer him or understand him, he just kept chatting away. Sometimes they could tell that he was talking about the places they were passing from the way he waved his arm out of the window, but what he was saying was a mystery.

Leda was happy just to listen to the man's foreign chatter and look out of the windows at the lovely mountain scenery. After about an hour the man stopped at a tiny little café for a late breakfast. The girls were relieved. They hadn't eaten since the middle of the last night, and they had walked miles since then. The smiled at the man, and Leda said "*efharisto*" again, the word for thank you. They sat outside on a terrace sheltered by vines, and ate double-baked bread with honey. It was delicious, and it was new to both of the girls. So was the coffee, which looked exactly the same as the Turkish coffee they were used to, but tasted different. When the waiter came for payment, Leda handed him all the notes she had. Her money covered the cost of the three breakfasts, but the waiter gave her only a couple of coins as change. Leda and Suela looked at each other in dismay. They didn't have money for any more food, and they didn't know where they could possibly get any more money from. But at least the transport was free, and the ride seemed more enjoyable now that they had full stomachs. The mountain roads gave way to flatter territory and towns. As the roads got less twisty both Leda and Suela dozed off, leaning against each other.

When they woke, they found that the car had stopped in a huge space like a car park. There were lots of other cars and lorries, and people standing around, and little caravans selling doughnuts. Ahead of them was a huge ferry which the cars and lorries were queuing up to get into. Leda had never seen a ship so large. What kind of a ship could carry *lorries*? She was so busy staring that she missed the Greek man offering something to her, and he had to wave them at her. It was a pair of tickets. Leda took them, wondering what they were for. The man was trying to tell her something, waving at the ship and pointing at them. Did he want them to leave? Wasn't he coming on the ship, too? Leda was really confused, but the man was pointing at her door so she got out, along with Suela. The man smiled, then waved her towards the ship. Leda and Suela weren't sure what was going on, but what could they do? They followed the queue of people towards the ship. Leda was afraid that the people checking the tickets might ask for passports, but they just tore off part of the ticket and waved the girls on. They climbed up the steep metal staircase along with everybody else, and discovered a deck with seats, and another deck above it, and even a restaurant inside. They were so busy exploring that they forgot about the Greek driver until he tapped them on the shoulder. He had come from another direction from them, and suddenly Leda understood – he had had to drive the car onto the ship, so he couldn't go in the same entrance as them. She was surprised at how pleased and relieved she was to see him again. She wanted to say so to Suela, but speaking Albanian seemed like a bad idea when there were so many people around.

Their driver found them a table, and then went off to the

bar. He came back with sandwiches for all of them, and fruit drinks. Leda tried to explain that she couldn't afford to pay him back by showing him her two small coins, but he just waved the money away. Leda said her only word of Greek again, and tucked in. At the other side of the stretch of water – Leda wasn't sure if it was a river or the sea – it was the same situation again. The girls got off first and waited for all the cars and lorries to shuffle their way out of the ship. Then they rejoined the Greek driver, and the journey continued.

It was afternoon by now, and Leda could tell they were going east because the sun was behind them, but she didn't know how Greece was laid out, so that didn't tell her where they were going. They passed through a few towns and a city, but neither of the girls had any idea if these would be good places to get off, so they just carried on travelling along with their good-natured, chatty chauffeur.

"At this rate," thought Leda, "We'll end up going home with him!" They changed direction after a while, and started going north. Leda saw some signs for Athens. They were hard to read in Greek, but it was a short word and she worked it out. The twisty mountain roads were hundreds of miles behind them, and now the man guided his car through big wide motorways and complicated junctions. Twice he had to stop to pay a toll for the road. These Athens roads were nothing like the girls had ever seen before, and Leda found herself feeling very out of place. Then, suddenly, she saw a name she recognised. The sign said ΛΑΥΡΙΟ, but Leda managed to work it out.

"Lavrio!" she said out loud. She turned to Suela to tell her that she had heard the emigrants talking about Lavrio, but she driver had heard her too.

"*Alvani, poli alvani,*" he said. He said a lot of other stuff that

Leda didn't understand, but she realised that *alvani* must mean Albanians or something like that. She almost laughed. All this time she and Suela had been trying not to talk in front of him so that he wouldn't realise that they had come from Albania, and he had known all along! Feeling free to talk now, she turned to Suela and explained that she had heard of Lavrio so there must be a lot of Albanians there. It seemed like a good place to finish their journey.

The kind Greek driver took the next turn-off for Lavrio, and in half an hour they were entering the seaside town. With its nice open square and greenery, Suela and Leda liked the look of it from the start. The driver pulled over and they all got out of the car. Leda wanted to thank him for being so kind, but all she could do was say *efharisto* lots of times and shake his hand. Suela did the same. The driver was still talking to them in Greek as he got back into the car, but just as he turned the engine on he seemed to remember something. He reached down to the floor in front of the passenger's seat, pulled something out and gave it to the girls. It was a calendar with lovely pictures of the countryside and words in Greek. As he passed it to Leda he said something, gesturing at the sky, and then at himself. He shrugged and smiled, acknowledging the language barrier between them. Then he pulled a couple of bank notes out of his pocket, and passed them to Leda. They tried to thank him again, but he was already pulling out. They waved goodbye as he went. Suela was amazed.

"Why did he help us so much? Do you think – do you think he was an angel?"

"No," said Leda, watching the car in the distance. "I think it's like Pastor Landi told me. Christians have brothers and sisters all over the world."

Chapter 19

So now they were in Lavrio – what should they do next? They probably didn't have enough money for a hotel, and they didn't know anyone they could stay with. They could buy something to eat with the money the man had given them, and it was already early evening, so they decided to have something to eat while they tried to make plans. They walked into the first café they saw, a kebab place that smelt very appetizing. The girls tried pointing at what they wanted on the menu, which had pictures, but the old man in the shop didn't understand them. He barked questions at them in Greek and tutted and sighed when they couldn't make any answer. Then he walked to the door and called along the street, something about *alvanika*. In a few moments a young man came in. Suela and Leda could see straight away that he was Albanian, although he was dressed just like a well-off Greek.

"This guy says you can't speak Greek. Are you Albanian?" the young man asked.

"Yes," said Leda, feeling a bit intimidated by his brusque attitude.

"So, what do you want to eat?" The girls gave their orders

and the young man told them the price.

"You should learn Greek," he said as he handed over the money, "It's no good trying to get by without it. How long have you been in the country?"

"About twenty-four hours!" said Leda. "We haven't had a chance to learn it yet. We came to Lavrio because there are Albanians here. I hoped I might be able to find out where my brother is – Geni Bektashi."

"Geni Bektashi?" said the intimidating young man, frowning. "I don't know him but I can ask around. Wait here." Then he walked out of the door, leaving them alone in the shop with the impatient old man. He finished making the kebabs and handed them to the girls, along with checked paper napkins. They had nearly finished their meal when a well-known face rushed into the shop. It was Geni's friend Berti.

"Leda!" said Berti, "and Suela! What on earth are you doing here? Have you come to see Geni? How did you get here?"

"Berti! Is Geni here?" said Leda, her heart racing with the thought of seeing her brother again.

"Of course he is, but he's down at the port buying tickets. A guy called Luani just told me there were two girls here asking about Geni so I thought I'd better come and find out who you were. You'd better come with me. Come on, we'll have to hurry or we'll miss the ferry."

"Ferry?" said Suela. "Where are we going?"

"To the island of Kea," said Berti. "Look, there's no time to explain now. Hurry up." He grabbed their rucksack and took off, with the girls running after him.

They ran down the hill towards the sea, then turned onto the road that ran beside the sea, towards the ferry. It was quite a long way and they were panting for breath when they arrived at the ferry's huge car park. There was a tiny little building in the middle of the car park with a queue of people waiting for tickets. Gasping, they kept running until they were in shouting distance of the ticket booth.

"Geni!" yelled Berti. "Two more tickets! Two more tickets!" The boy at the front of the queue looked round, and Leda's heart leapt. He was taller and stronger than the last time she had seen him, and he had dyed his hair with blonde streaks, but it was definitely Geni. He saw her too, and his mouth fell open with surprise. He forgot what he was doing until the woman in the booth asked him again for his order. He spoke in Greek, paid the money, waited impatiently for the four tickets to be printed out, then ran over to the group.

"Leda!" he said, hugging her hard. "How on earth did you get here? How are Mami and Babi? And Suela, you're here too?" He gave her a hug, too. Leda was about to start telling him the story of how they had come to be here, but Berti interrupted.

"Look, if we don't get on that ferry now we'll be staying in Lavrio tonight. It's the last ferry. You can talk once we're on board." They knew Berti was right, so they rushed down to the ferry and climbed the steep metal stairs up to the deck.

It was getting cooler now that it was evening, so they sat indoors in the café. They got a table next to a window, and Leda could see the land seeming to move as the ferry started to get going. Berti went to get drinks and crisps for them all, and Suela went with him to help carry them, so Leda and Geni were left alone. He took her hands. He looked wonderful – healthy, well-fed, not at all the poor starving immigrant she had worried about.

"Leda," he said. "It's wonderful to see you again. But how

did you get here? And why did you leave Albania?" So Leda started to tell him the whole story about her father taking her out of school, and Mr Gjoni, and the violent riots with guns, and Maks wanting to sell Suela. Berti and Suela came back with the drinks, and the two boys listened in amazement as they girls told the story of how they had come over the mountains into Greece. Leda told them about the kind Greek man who had helped them, and she unrolled the calendar to show them.

"'You will keep in perfect peace him whose mind is steadfast because his trust is in you.' Isaiah 26, verse 3," read Geni, holding the calendar.

"What?" said Leda, stunned.

"This is a Christian calendar he's given you. It's got Bible verses on it in Greek. They were giving the exact same calendars out at my church."

"Your church?" said Leda.

"Yes, I go the Albanian-speaking church near Lavrio. Somebody on Kea told me about it, and I wanted to go somewhere where everyone spoke Albanian, so I started going and – well, you know – I found out about Jesus and I became a Christian. So now I go just about every week. That's why we were over in Lavrio today, because of church – it's Sunday."

Leda leaned across the table and threw her arms round her brother.

"Geni, that's wonderful! I'll have to tell you all about the new pastor in our village! But first, tell us about what you've been doing, what job you've got, how you ended up on this island, where you're living, everything!"

Geni laughed. "You're not on the run any more, girls. You'll have all the time you want to hear about my boring job as a builder, and *my* trip over the mountains last year. And as

for where I live, you live there too now! We're family, after all."
He smiled at his sister as the ferry rocked gently across the sea towards the quiet island.

"Welcome home, Leda."

Epilogue

Pastor Landi Rama sighed as he sat down at his desk in the little church in Mallakaster. He was so tired! He had spent all morning trying to find places for the newly arrived refugees to stay, and he knew that more would probably arrive tomorrow. He rubbed the back of his neck. His head was aching with the stress and all the running around. War had broken out in Kosovo between the Serbs and the Albanians. It was a nasty, brutal war. It wasn't just the soldiers who were involved, all citizens were in danger. So the Albanians in Kosovo had started fleeing south into Albania, hoping to find safety. Kosovo was north of Albania, but there were so many refugees that lots of them had had to keep going further and further south to find places which would take them in, and so they had finally arrived in Mallakaster, causing Pastor Landi's headache.

There were also their children to think about. Parents had brought their children into Albania with them, to keep them safe. Now the kids had nothing to do, no school to go to, many of them only had one parent with them, and a lot of them had never been told about Jesus in their lives. The church was helping out as much as they could, but it was a small church and there was only so much they could do. It was good that the church members had taken the refugees into their homes, but how could he ask them to do more? Landi picked up a pencil and started making a list of things that needed to be done. Visits to the refugees, extra money for food for the families who had taken them in, some kind of children's club… He wondered if some of the larger churches in Tirana could help, and perhaps foreign churches could provide money to look after the refugees. He wrote another list of people he should phone to talk about these things.

Just then there was a knock at the door. Landi wasn't happy to be interrupted when he had only just got some time to himself, but he put down the pencil and tried to be welcoming.

"Come in," he said, cheerfully. A young woman walked into his office. She was smart and well-dressed, and she was smiling at him as if she knew him. Landi looked more closely and realised that she *did* look familiar. He was trying to think of her name, and where he'd seen her before, when she beat him to it.

"Pastor Landi, don't you remember me? It's Leda Bektashi!" Suddenly he remembered. Leda, the girl from the mountain village. She had disappeared one day a couple of years ago, at the start of the riots over the pyramid scheme, and she had never come back. He had heard that she had called her parents to say that she, Suela and her brother were all okay, and that they were living in Greece, but he didn't have any more details and he couldn't ask her parents. Her father thought that religion was the reason she had run away, and he wouldn't talk to Landi or let his wife talk to him either. And now here she was, two years later, standing in his office!

Landi pulled over another chair for Leda and put the kettle

on for coffee. He was so excited to hear about her news that he forgot to ask why she had come. She and Suela had been working as waitresses on Kea, living with Geni and Suela. Suela was engaged to Berti, and they would be getting married in the summer. Leda had plans, too. At first she had struggled with Greek, but she had tried hard and now she was so good that she was going to go to a Greek Bible school in the autumn.

"It's in Athens, so it's not too far. I can stay with a Greek pastor and his wife there, and go back to Kea at the weekends," she explained. She paused for a moment. "But of course I heard about the war in Kosovo and all the refugees, and I came back to see if I could do anything. I've been granted my papers to stay in Greece, so I can come and go now, you see. So, is there anything I can do?" Pastor Landi couldn't believe his ears. He had been praying for someone to help him, and now God had sent him help in the most unexpected way.

"Thank you, God!" he said out loud. Then he turned to Leda and said, "Can you help? There's so much you can do! Would you like a list?"

A couple of days later, Leda found herself facing a room full of Kosovar children, with some local children mixed in with them. There was a lot of noise, and she could hear the strange, thick accents of the refugees as they chattered to each other. Leda was a bit nervous, but she tried to concentrate on what she was doing, setting up her laptop. She put the DVD in the drive, pushed it in, and got the film ready to play. Then she turned to the room full of children.

"Quieten down, all of you!" she shouted over the noise. "I've got a special film to show you. I saw this years ago and the star of the film has been a friend of mine ever since. He's taken me through some difficult situations and always kept me safe.

He's never let me down. Today I want to introduce you all to him."

Leda clicked the mouse and the film started playing, the same film she had watched sitting on the ground in her village one summer evening all those years ago.

"I want to introduce you to Jesus."

Acknowledgements

Thanks go to Dayspring Jubilee McLeod, my patient copy editor; Lillian Miller and Gordon Thomason for their tireless support; Dr John Blanchard for his willingness to help me out; and many of my Albanian friends and relatives whose stories I have plundered shamelessly for background detail. Thanks also go, of course, to an old Friend that I met many years ago, when I was even younger than Leda.